An Introduction to LINGUISTICS

Language, Grammar and Semantics

SECOND EDITION

PUSHPINDER SYAL
Professor, Department of English
Panjab University, Chandigarh

D.V. JINDAL
Former Faculty Member, Postgraduate Department of English
Government College, Ludhiana

PHI Learning Private Limited
Delhi-110092
2023

₹ 250.00

AN INTRODUCTION TO LINGUISTICS: Language, Grammar and Semantics, 2nd ed.
Pushpinder Syal and D.V. Jindal

ISBN-978-81-203-3216-4 (Print Book)
ISBN-978-93-90669-23-3 (e-Book)

Published by Asoke K. Ghosh, PHI Learning Private Limited, Rimjhim House, 111, Patparganj Industrial Estate, Delhi-110092 and Printed by Mudrak, D-61, Sector 63, Noida, U.P.-201301.

Contents

SECTION II: THE STUDY OF GRAMMAR

Preface

For several years, this book has proved to be useful to students who wanted an introduction to Linguistics, Grammar and Semantics. The requirement of the students was, and is, for a book that familiarizes them with a new subject and creates interest in studying it further.

In order to make this book even more comprehensive, we have now added a couple of new chapters and made some additions in the existing ones. A new chapter on Language Variation (Chapter 5) deals with some important terms such as dialect, accent, and stylistics, and gives instances of varieties of English around the world. One more new chapter (Chapter 11) on Supra-sentential Grammar covering rules of cohesion and linkage, which is a **must** for the study of linguistics today, has been added.

We hope these additions as well as other modifications to the text will add to the usefulness of this book for students. We are grateful to Professor J. Sethi, former Professor, Central Institute of English and Foreign Languages, Hyderabad, and an accomplished writer himself, for taking the time to comment on the revisions.

Pushpinder Syal
D.V. Jindal

Preface

Preface to the First Edition

This book is intended for Indian students in various universities and institutes of languages who take up an introductory course in Linguistics. It aims at introducing basic concepts in Linguistics and familiarising students with the fundamentals of modern Linguistics in a clear and simple manner. The objective of the book is to facilitate the grasp of ideas in Linguistics to students new in the discipline, as a stepping stone to further reading in the subject.

The topics covered in the book correspond generally to those included in most introductory courses in Linguistics. Accordingly, the book has been divided into three sections. Section I is an introduction to the study of language, dealing with definitions, scope of enquiry, and concepts in Linguistics. Section II deals with the basics of modern grammar, and Section III introduces semantics. The style which is adopted throughout the book is that of discussion and exemplification. The chapter summaries provide a quick revision of main points and the questions at the end of each chapter help to test understanding as well as to initiate further discussion. Though most of the examples in grammar and semantics are based on the structure of the English language, students must note that the principles of language study as discussed here are applicable to all languages, and we would certainly like to make the suggestion that students and teachers try out some of the methods of analysis in describing and analysing structures in their own languages. We would welcome comments and ideas from teachers and students to enable us to make the book more useful.

We wish to express our gratitude to Dr. J. Sethi, former Professor of Phonetics, Central Institute of English and Foreign Languages, Hyderabad, who has been the guiding spirit of this work and has made special efforts to enable us in bringing out the book in its present form. Finally, we would like to thank our families for their encouragement and support.

Pushpinder Syal
D.V. Jindal

SECTION I

The Study of Language

CHAPTER 1

Language

1.1 WHAT IS LANGUAGE?

Everybody knows the answer to this question but nobody has so far been able to come out with any standard definition that fully explains the term **language**. It is a situation like trying to define the term **life**. Everybody knows what life is but one cannot present a satisfactory definition of life. In order to understand a term like 'life', one has to talk of the properties or characteristics of living beings (e.g. motion, reproduction, respiration, growth, power of self-healing, excretion, nutrition, mortality, etc.). Similarly, the term 'language' can be understood better in terms of its properties or characteristics. Some linguists, however, have been trying to define language in their own ways even though all these definitions are far from satisfactory. Here are some of these definitions:

1. Language is a symbol system based on pure or arbitrary conventions... infinitely extendable and modifiable according to the changing needs and conditions of the speakers.

Robins (1985)

According to this definition, language is a symbol system. Every language (that exists in the written form) selects some symbols for its selected sounds. For the sound /k/, in English we have the symbol k and in Hindi we have क. These symbols form the alphabet of the language and join in different combinations (according to a well laid out system) to form meaningful words.

The system talked of here is purely arbitrary in the sense that there is no one to one correspondence between the structure of a word and the thing it stands for. The combination of letters **p.e.n.**, for example stands, in English, for an instrument used for writing. Why could it not be **e.p.n.** or **n.e.p.**? Well, it could also be **e.p.n.** or **n.e.p.**, and there is nothing sacrosanct about the combination **p.e.n.** except that it has now become a convention—a convention that cannot be easily changed.

As stated here, language conventions are not easily changed, yet it is not impossible to do so. Language is infinitely modifiable and extendable. Words go on changing meanings and new words continue to be added to language with the changing needs of the community using it. Shakespeare, for example, used the word **stomach** to mean **courage**. Similarly words like **laser, sputnik, and astronaut** are of quite recent origin in the English language.

2. Language is a purely human and non-instinctive method of communicating ideas, emotions and desires by means of a system of voluntarily produced symbols.

Sapir (1921)

There are two terms in this definition that call for discussion: **human** and **non-instinctive**. Language, as Sapir rightly said, is human. Only humans possess language and all normal humans uniformly possess it. Animals do have a communication system but it is not a developed system. That is why language is said to be **species-specific** and **species-uniform**.

Also, language does not pass from a parent to a child. In this sense, it is non-instinctive. A child has to learn language and he/she learns the language of the society he/she is placed in.

3. Language is the institution whereby humans communicate and interact with each other by means of habitually used oral-auditory arbitrary symbols.

Hall (1969)

This definition rightly gives more prominence to the fact that language is primarily speech produced by oral-auditory symbols. A speaker produces some string of oral sounds that get conveyed through the air to the listener who, through his hearing organs, receives the sound waves and conveys these to the brain that interprets these symbols to arrive at a meaning.

4. A language is a set (finite or infinite) of sentences, each finite in length and constructed out of a finite set of elements.

Noam Chomsky (1957)

Chomsky meant to convey that each sentence has a structure. Human brain is competent enough to construct different sentences from out of the limited set of sounds/symbols belonging to a particular language. Human brain is so productive that a child can at any time produce a sentence that has never been said or heard earlier.

5. A language is a system of arbitrary vocal symbols used for human communication.

Wardaugh (1972)

6. A language is a system of arbitrary vocal symbols by means of which a social group cooperates.

Bloch and Trager (1942)

Both the definitions 5 and 6 above prominently point out that language is a **system**. Sounds join to form words according to a system. The letters k, n, i, t join to form a meaningful word **knit**, whereas combinations like n-k-i-t, t.k.n.i. or i.n.k.t. do not form any meaningful or sensible combinations. As said earlier, although initially the formation of words, is only arbitrary, convention makes them parts of a system. Words too join to form sentences according to some system. A sentence like: **Cricket is a game of glorious uncertainties** is acceptable but one cannot accept a string of words like: *a game is of cricket uncertainties glorious*. It is in this sense that language is said to be a **system of systems**.

7. Language is undoubtedly a kind of means of communication among human beings. It consists primarily of vocal sounds. It is articulatory, systematic, symbolic and arbitrary.

Derbyshire (1967)

Derbyshire, while accepting that language is the property of human beings and that it is primarily speech, brings out the point that it is an important means of communication amongst humans. Before the start of civilization, man might have used the language of signs, but it must have had a very limited scope. Language is a fully developed means of communication with the civilized man who can convey and receive millions of messages across the universe. An entire civilization depends on language only. Think of a world without language—man would only continue to be a denizen of the forest and the caves. Language has changed the entire gamut of human relations and made it possible for human beings to grow into a human community on this planet.

1.11 Some More Definitions

8. Language is a system of conventional spoken or written symbols by means of which human beings, as members of a social group and participants in its culture, communicate.

Encyclopaedia Britannica

9. Languages are the principal systems of communication used by particular groups of human beings within the particular society (linguistic community) of which they are members.

Lyons (1970)

It is clearly evident from all these definitions, none of which completely defines the term 'language', that it is not possible to have a single definition that brings out all the properties of language. On the basis of these definitions, one can, however, list out the various characteristics of language. It would, therefore, be better to list these characteristics and discuss them in detail.

1.2 CHARACTERISTICS OF LANGUAGE

1.21 Language is a Means of Communication

Language is a very important means of communication between humans. **A** can communicate his or her ideas, emotions, beliefs or feelings to **B** as they share a common code that makes up the language. No doubt, there are many other means of communication used by humans, e.g. gestures, nods, winks, flags, smiles, horns, short-hand, braille alphabet, mathematical symbols, morse code, sirens, sketches, maps, acting, miming, dancing, and so on. But all these systems of communication are extremely limited or they too, in turn, depend language only. They are not so flexible, comprehensive, perfect and extensive as language is. Language is so important a form of communication between humans that it is difficult to think of a society without language. It gives shape to people's thoughts, and guides and controls their entire activity. It is a carrier of civilization and culture as human thoughts and philosophy are conveyed from one generation to the other through the medium of language. Language is ubiquitous in the sense that it is present everywhere in all activities. It is as important as the air we breathe and is the most valuable possession of man. In the scheme of things, all humans are blessed with language and it is the specific property of humans only. Language is thus species-specific and species-uniform. It is because of the use of language that humans are called "talking animals" (*Homo loquens*).

Animals too have their system of communication but their communication is limited to a very small number of messages, e.g. hunger, and thirst, fear and anger. In the case of humans, the situation is entirely different. Human beings can send an infinite number of messages to their fellow beings. It is through language that they store knowledge, transfer it to the next generation and yoke the present, past and the future together.

1.22 Language is Arbitrary

Language is arbitrary in the sense that there is no inherent relation between the words of a language and their meanings or the ideas conveyed by them (except in the case of hieroglyphics, where a picture of an object may represent the object). There is no reason why a female adult human being be called a **woman** in English, *istree* in Hindi, *aurat* in Urdu, *Zen* in Persian, *Femine* in French or *tinvi* in Punjabi. Selection of these words in the languages mentioned here is purely arbitrary, an accident of history. It is just like christening a new born baby John or James. But once a child is given some name in a purely arbitrary manner, this name gets associated with the child for his entire life and it becomes an important, established convention. The situation in the case of language is a similar one. The choice of a word selected to mean a particular thing or idea is purely arbitrary, but once a word is selected for a particular referent, it comes to stay as such.

It may be noted that had language not been arbitrary, there would have been only one language in the world.

The arbitrary nature of language permits or presupposes change, but such changes do not normally take place. Names once given are not normally changed. Words in a language are more difficult to change because a whole society has accepted them. Therefore, while the arbitrary nature of language permits change, its conventionality gives it stability.

There are words in some languages, which do have a relation with the meanings or ideas they stand for. *Onomatopoeia* is a term used for words that imitate the sounds they stand for, e.g. *bang, thud, buzz, hum*. But such words are very few, and for the same sound, different languages have different words. These words, therefore, do not invalidate the fact that words in a language are arbitrarily selected and that the relationship between words and their referents is purely arbitrary.

1.23 Language is a System of Systems

Language is not an amorphous, disorganised or chaotic combination of sounds. Any brick may be used anywhere in a building, but it is not so with sounds or graphic symbols standing for the sounds of a language. Sounds are arranged in certain fixed or established, systematic order to form meaningful units or words. Similarly, words are also arranged in a particular system to frame acceptable meaningful sentences. These systems operate at two levels: phonological and syntactical.

At the phonological level, for example, the sounds of a language appear only in some fixed combinations. There is no word, for example, that starts with bz–, lr– or zl– combination. Again, while there are several English words having an initial consonant cluster with three consonants (e.g. spring/string), there are no initial tetraphonemic consonant clusters (a string of four consonants in the same syllable) in English. There is no word that begins with a /N/ sound or ends in a /h/ sound*. Similarly, words too combine to form sentences according to certain conventions (i.e. grammatical or structural rules) of the language. The sentence "The hunter shot the tiger with a gun" is acceptable but the sentence "hunter the tiger a shot gun with the" is not acceptable as the word order in the latter sentence does not conform to the established language conventions.

Language is thus called a *system of systems* as it operates at the two levels discussed above. This property of language is also termed **duality** by some linguists. This makes language a very complex phenomenon. Every human child has to master the conventions of the language he or she learns before being able to successfully communicate with other members of the social group in which he or she is placed.

1.24 Language is Primarily Vocal

Language is primarily made up of vocal sounds only, produced by a physiological articulatory mechanism in the human body. In the beginning, it must have appeared as vocal sounds only. Writing must have come much later, as an intelligent attempt to represent vocal sounds. Writing is the graphic representation of the sounds of the language. The letters **k** or **q** represent only the /k/ sound. Graphic symbols had to be invented for the sake of some sounds. There are a number of languages which continue to exist, even today, in the spoken form only. They do not have a written form. A child learns to speak first; writing comes much later. Also, during his lifetime, a man speaks much more than he writes. The total quantum of speech is much larger than the total quantum of written materials.

It is because of these reasons that modern linguists say that speech is primary, writing is secondary. Writing did have one advantage over speech—it could be preserved in books or records. But, with the invention of magnetic tapes or audio-cassettes, it has lost that advantage too. A number of modern gadgets like the telephone, the tape recorder, the dictaphone, etc. prove the primacy of speech over writing in the present time.

1.25 Language Differs from Animal Communication in Several Ways

Language is primarily human. It is humans alone that possess language and use it for communication. Language is, in that sense, **species-specific**—it is specific

* the word **ah** is pronounced */a:/*
the word **oh** is pronounced */əʊ/*

only to one set of species. Also, all human beings uniformly possess language. It is only a few deaf (and therefore dumb) persons who cannot speak. Thus language is **species-uniform** to that extent. Animals also have their own system of communication but communication between them is extremely limited. It is limited to a very small number of messages. *Animal communication differs from human communication in the following ways*:

(a) Language can convey a large number, rather an infinite set, of messages whereas the number of messages conveyed through the communication system of animals is very limited. Animals, for example, are able to convey to their fellow animals if they are hungry or afraid. A bee, by its dance, is able to convey the distance or the direction of the source of nectar, but it cannot convey how good or bad this honey is. Similarly, a bee cannot tell another bee that the source of honey is 10 metres to the left of a point 15 metres to the right. Language can thus convey messages along several directions whereas, in the case of bees, messages are differentiated along two dimensions only, i.e., direction and distance. Some monkeys, it is known, can produce a number of (not more than 9 to 10) sounds to express fear, aggression, anger, love, etc., but these messages too are extremely limited in number.

(b) Language makes use of clearly distinguishable discrete, separately identifiable symbols while animal communication systems are often continuous or non-discrete.

One can clearly distinguish between /k/, /æ/ and /t/ in the word **cat**, but one

Fig. 1.1 Language is discrete.

cannot identify different discrete symbols in the long humming sound that a bee produces or the 'caw-caw' sound of a crow.

(c) Animal communication systems are closed systems that permit of no change, modification or addition. A bee's dance or a cock's crow is today the same that it was 200 years ago. It is not so in the case of language. Language is changing, growing every day, and new words continue to be added to it in the course of time. Words like **sputnik**, **laser**, **video**, **software** did not, for example, exist anywhere in English language 300 years ago. Language is thus open ended, modifiable and extendable.

(d) Human language is far more structurally complex than animal communication. English (RP variety), for example, has 44 sounds that join in different groups to form thousands of words. These words can be arranged into millions of sets to frame different sentences. Each sentence has its own internal structure. There is no such structural complexity in a lamb's bleating or a monkey's cry.

(e) Human language is non-instinctive in the sense that every human child has to **learn** language from his elders or peers in society. This process of **learning** plays an important part in the acquisition of language. On the other hand, bees acquire their skill in dancing as humans acquire the skill to walk. They are sometimes seen to make hexagonal hives. They do not learn any geometry. Their knowledge is inherited, inbuilt. It is not so in the case of human beings who have to **learn** a language.

(f) **Displacement**. Animal communication, as in the case of communication system in birds, dogs, monkeys, insects etc., is limited to or related to their immediate time and place, here and now or near about. It does not contain any information about the past or the future or about the events taking place in the distant multidimensional set-up. When your pet animal produces a sound, a cat mews or a dog barks, you understand the message as relating to your immediate present and place at the moment. It cannot tell you where it was two days ago or where it would be in the evening or what it was up to in the next few minutes. Human language users are capable of producing messages pertaining to the present, past or future, near or distant places, i.e. in a multidimensional setting. One can say, for example:

> I was 200 km north of New York last month but will be deep down in the south of America next week. I witnessed a Rugby match in September last but will be an umpire in the one-day cricket match at the Mohali cricket ground.

This property is called **displacement**. It allows the users of language to talk about things and events which are not present in the immediate environment of the speaker. Animal communication lacks this property.

Even if some animals do display this property of displacement in their communication system, the messages are extremely limited. A honeybee can, for example, convey the distance and the direction of the source of nectar, but it cannot tell another bee that it should first turn right for a distance of 10 metres and then fly across the left wall into a well in the rose garden on the east. The property of displacement in human language enables us to talk even of things, persons or events that are non-existent or imaginary or are likely to be found on other planets. We can talk of a superman, test-tube babies, artificial limbs, havocs of war, fairies, angels, demons, the spiderman, Santa Claus and the like. It is this property of displacement that allows humans to create, for example, literature, fiction, fantasy or the stream of consciousness stories.

1.26 Language is a Form of Social Behaviour

As already stated above, language has to be learnt. This learning is possible only in society. A human child learns to speak the language of the community or the group in which he or she is placed. A Chinese infant, if placed in an Indian family, will easily learn to speak an Indian language. He or she picks up the language of the social set-up in which he or she grows. Language is thus a form of social behaviour.

1.27 Language is a Symbol System

A symbol is a concrete event, object or mark that stands for something relatively abstract. The cross (+), for example, is a symbol that stands for the great sacrifice of Jesus Christ, i.e., his suffering and death on the cross; it is also a symbol of a Christian. Similarly, words are symbols that stand for objects. The symbol/teɪbl/ stands for an object consisting of a wooden-board supported by four/three legs. A speaker or a writer wants to communicate with another fellow-being, puts his message across in the form of symbols (in speech or writing). The receiver of the message, who shares a common code with the sender of the message, decodes this message sent in the form of symbols and interprets these to arrive at a certain meaning. Thus language is a symbol system, though different languages use different symbols.

1.28 Productivity

Language is creative and productive in the sense that a user of a language does not always produce only sentences that he has heard or learnt previously. On the basis of his 'knowledge' of the grammar and syntax of the language, he can always produce new sentences, write new poems or produce many other kinds of new literature. He can produce an infinite number of sentences as per the eventuality he is facing within the framework of the grammar of the language being used by him. This property of language is called **Productivity**.

1.29 Interchangeability

It is an important characteristic of human language that it permits a speaker to become a listener and vice versa without impairing the function of language, i.e. communication. This property has been named Interchangeability by C.F. Hockett (*A Course in Modern Linguistics*). It can also be called **reciprocity**, i.e. any speaker/sender of a linguistic signal can also be a listener/receiver.

1.3 WHY STUDY LANGUAGE?

Having outlined the various characteristics of language, one may like to ask: why study or learn language at all? An answer to this question can be easily derived from a consideration of the situation this world was in before language came into existence. One can easily imagine that man must then have been a denizen of the forest very much like anyone of the other animals, viz. horse, cow, tiger, elephant, and dog. The entire human progress, in fact everything that distinguishes humans from animals, depends on language only. Language is, today, a medium of literature, science and technology, computers and cultural exchanges between social groups, and the most powerful, convenient and permanent means of communication in the world. It is ubiquitous, present everywhere in all human activities, thoughts, dreams, prayers, meditations and relations. It is only through language that knowledge and culture are stored and passed on from generation to generation. Thus, all human civilization and knowledge are possible only through language.

SUMMARY

It is as difficult to define the term **language** as it is to define the term **life.** Just as **life** can be defined only in terms of certain characteristics (growth, reproduction, excretion, respiration, etc.), language can also be defined in terms of its characteristics. Various linguists have tried to define language in their own ways but one would like to list all the characteristics of language as contained in these definitions. Here are the various characteristics or properties of language:

1. Language is a means of communication.
2. Language is arbitrary.
3. Language is a system of systems.
4. Language is primarily vocal. Speech is primary; writing is secondary.
5. Language is human. It differs from animal communication in several ways:
   (a) Humans convey and receive an infinite number of messages through space whereas animal communication system is extremely limited and undeveloped.
   (b) Language makes use of clearly distinguishable, discrete, separately identifiable symbols while animal communication systems are often continuous and non-discrete.
   (c) Animal communication systems are closed systems and permit no change whereas language is modifiable, extendable and open-ended.
   (d) Human language is structurally more complex than animal communication system.
6. Language is a form of social behaviour.
7. Language is a symbol system.

Language is, today, an inseparable part of human society. Human civilization has been possible only through language. It is through language that humanity has come out of the stone age and has developed science, art and technology in a big way.

COMPREHENSION QUESTIONS

1. What are the various definitions of the term **language**?

2. List the various characteristics of language. Explain any two of these.

3. How does language differ from animal communication?

4. Write short notes on the following:

   (a) Language is arbitrary.
   (b) Language is a system of systems.
   (c) Speech is primary, writing is secondary.
   (d) Language is open-ended, modifiable and extendable depending on the needs of the people using it.

(e) Language is a means of communication.
(f) Language is species-specific and species-uniform.

5. Fill up the blanks:
   (a) There is ________ one-to-one correspondence between a word and the thing it stands for.
   (b) Human language is discrete, while animal communication is ________.
   (c) Speech is ________, but writing is ________.
   (d) Language is a system of systems. This property of language is also called ________.
   (e) Language does not automatically pass on from one generation to the other. It has to be ________ by practice.

CHAPTER 2

What is Linguistics?

2.1 DEFINITION

Linguistics is the scientific study of language. The word 'language' here means language in general, not a particular language. If we were concerned with studying an individual language, we would say "I'm studying French... or English," or whichever language we happen to be studying. But linguistics does not study an individual language, it studies 'language' in general. According to Robins (1985), linguistics

> is concerned with human language as a universal and recognizable part of the human behaviour and of the human faculties perhaps one of the most essential to human life as we know it, and one of the most far-reaching of human capabilities in relation to the whole span of mankind's achievements.

Does this not sound a little abstract? It is, because there is no way of studying 'language' without referring to and taking examples from particular languages. However, even while doing so, the emphasis of linguistics is different. Linguistics does not emphasise practical knowledge or mastery of a particular language. Linguists may know only one language, or may know several, or may even study a language they do not know at all. They try to study the ways in which language is organised to fulfil human needs, as a system of communication. There is a difference between a person who knows many languages (called a **polyglot**), and a **linguist**, who studies general principles of language organisation and language behaviour, often with reference to some actual language or languages. Any language can be taken up to illustrate the principles of language organisation, because all languages reveal something of the nature of language in general. (Of course, it may be of help to a linguist to know more languages so that differences and contrasts as well as similarities between the languages can also be studied in a better way.)

We can say that linguistics is learning **about** language rather than learning **a** language. This distinction is often explained as the difference between learning how a car works and learning how to drive a car. When we learn how to drive a car, we learn a set of habits and do some practice—this is similar to learning how to speak a language. When we learn how the car works, we open up its mechanism, study it and investigate the relationship of its parts to one another. This is similar to what we do in a scientific study of language, or linguistics: we investigate the mechanism of language, its parts, and how all these parts fit together to perform particular functions, and why they are arranged or organised in a certain manner. Just as while driving a car we are using its various components, while speaking a language we are using the sounds, words, etc. of that language; behind these uses is the mechanism which enables us to do so. We study language because it is important for us to understand this mechanism.

Every language is a system; so it does not matter which language we take up to illustrate the working of 'language' in human life. In earlier times, the study of language was considered to be the study of the grammar of some prestigious or classical language such as Latin, Sanskrit, or Greek. Today we consider all languages as fit objects of language study.

2.2 LINGUISTICS AS A SCIENCE

Linguistics can be understood as a science, in both general and specific terms. Generally, we use the term 'science' for any knowledge that is based on clear, systematic and rational understanding. Thus we often speak of the 'science of politics' or statecraft, or 'the science of cooking'. However, we also use the term 'science' for the systematic study of phenomena, enabling us to state some principles or theories regarding the phenomena. This study proceeds by examination of publicly verifiable data obtained through observation of phenomena, and experimentation; in other words, it is **empirical and objective**. Science must also provide explanation after adequate observation of data, which should be **consistent,** i.e. there should be no contradiction between different parts of the explanation or statement; and **economical**, i.e. a precise and non-redundant statement is to be preferred.

Let us apply these criteria of science to linguistics. Linguistics studies language: language is a phenomenon which is both objective and variable. Like natural phenomena in the physical world, like organisms in the living world, it has a concrete shape and occurrence. In the same way as a physicist or chemist takes materials and measures their weights, densities etc. to determine their nature, and in the same way as a biologist takes a specimen of some form of life and examines it under a microscope, the linguist studies the components of language, e.g. observing the occurrence of speech-sounds, or the way in which words begin or end. Language, like other phenomena, is objective because it is observable with the senses, i.e., it can be heard with the ear, it can be seen when the vocal organs are in movement, or when reading words on a page.

Observation leads to processes of classification and definition. In science, each observable phenomenon is to be given a precise explanation. Its nature has to be described completely. Thus, for example, the chemist classifies elements into metals and non-metals; a biologist classifies living beings into plants and animals; further classifications are then made according to the characteristics of the objects belonging to a particular class, sub class, etc. Similarly, linguistics observes the features of language, classifies these features as being sound features of particular types, or words belonging to particular classes on the basis of similarity or difference with other sounds and words.

But while linguistics shares some of the characteristics of empirical science, it is also a social science because it studies language which is a form of social behaviour and exists in interaction between human beings in society. Language is also linked to human mental processes. For these reasons, it cannot be treated always as objective phenomena.

In empirical sciences, the methods of observation and experimentation are known as inductive procedures. This means that phenomena are observed and data collected without any preconceived idea or theory, and after the data are studied, some theory is formulated. This has been the main tradition in the history of western science. But there is also the opposite tradition—the tradition of rationalism—which holds that the mind forms certain concepts or ideas beforehand in terms of which it interprets the data of observation and experience. According to this tradition, the deductive procedure is employed in which we have a preliminary hypothesis or theory in our minds. We try to prove this hypothesis by applying it to the data. This procedure was considered to be unscientific according to the empirical scientists because they felt that pre-existent ideas can influence the kind of data we obtain, i.e. we search only for those pieces of data that fit our theory and disregard others and, therefore, it is not an objective method. On the other hand, it has been observed by some thinkers (such as Karl Popper) that no observation can be free of some theory; it cannot be totally neutral.

We can, however, reconcile these two procedures. There are aspects of language which we can observe quite easily and which offer concrete instances of objective and verifiable data. At the same time, we need to create a tentative or working hypothesis to explain this data, which we may accept, reject or modify as we proceed further. With such an open attitude, we may collect more data. This alternation of inductive and deductive procedures may help us to arrive at explanations which meet all the requirements of science, i.e. they are exhaustive, consistent and concise.

Thus, linguistics is both an empirical science and a social science. In fact, it is a human discipline since it is concerned with human language; so it is part of the study of humanities as well. This includes the study of literature, and appreciation of the beauty and music of poetry. In understanding language, humankind can understand itself. Moreover, since every branch of knowledge uses language, linguistics is central to all areas of knowledge. The traditional distinctions of science, art and humanities are not relevant for linguistics. As Lyons puts it, linguistics has natural links with a wide range of academic disciplines. To say that linguistics is a science is not to deny that, by virtue of its subject matter, it is closely related to such eminently human disciplines as philosophy and literary criticism (Lyons, 1981, p. 45).

2.3 SCOPE OF LINGUISTICS

Linguistics today is a subject of study, independent of other disciplines. Before the twentieth century, the study of language was not regarded as a separate area of study in its own right. It was considered to be a part of studying the history of language or the philosophy of language, and this was known not as linguistics but as philosophy. So, 'Linguistics' is a modern name which defines a specific discipline, in which we study language not in relation to some other area such as history or philosophy, but language as itself, as a self-enclosed and autonomous system, worthy of study in its own right. It was necessary at the beginning of the growth of modern linguistics to define this autonomy of the subject; otherwise, it would not have been possible to study the language system with the depth and exhaustiveness which it requires. However, now we acknowledge that while linguistics is a distinct area of study, it is also linked to other disciplines and there are overlapping areas of concern.

The main concern of modern linguistics is to describe language, to study its nature, and to establish a theory of language. That is, it aims at studying the components of the language system and to ultimately arrive at an explanatory statement on how the system works. In modern linguistics, the activity of describing the language system is most important, and so modern linguistics is generally known as *descriptive*. But linguistics has other concerns as well, which fall within its scope, and these include historical and comparative study of language. These differ from the descriptive approach in their emphasis; otherwise, these approaches also involve description of language. They are discussed in detail below.

2.31 Descriptive, Comparative and Historical Linguistics

From Robins (1985, p. 3), we have the definition:

> Descriptive linguistics is concerned with the description and analysis of the ways in which a language operates and is used by a given set of speakers at a given time.

This time may be the present or the past at a given time, the language is described irrespective of what preceded it or may follow it.

Descriptive linguistics is emphasized in modern linguistics as it is the fundamental aspect of the study of language. It contrasts with prescriptive linguistics of earlier times, because it deals with description of how language actually works, rather than how it should be; in itself rather than in relation to other languages. In descriptive linguistics, we describe the language systematically at **all** levels, i.e. phonology, grammar and semantics. We analyse and describe the structure of the language. Modern descriptive linguistics is based on a **structural approach** to language, as exemplified in the work of Bloomfield and others (see Chapter 4).

With regard to historical linguistics, Robins (1985, p. 5) explains:

> Historical linguistics is the study of the developments in languages in the course of time, the ways in which languages change from period to period and of the causes and results of such changes... it must be based on a description of two or more stages in the development of the language being studied.

The terms **synchronic** and **diachronic** given by Saussure (1916) are used to distinguish between the description of a stage of a language at a given time and the description of changes that take place in language during the passage of time.

> A synchronic description is non-historical, a diachronic description traces the historical development of a language (Lyons, 1981, p. 219).

If we study the changes that have taken place in English from Old English to Middle English and to Modern English, it is a diachronic (or historical) study. If we study the structure of English as it exists today and describe it without reference to how it was used in the past, it is synchronic study (Also see Chapter 3 for explanation of this distinction). Comparative linguistics is concerned with comparing two or more languages. When the history of these languages is compared with a view to discovering the historical relation between these languages, it is known as comparative historical study (or philosophy). This kind of study was dominant in the 19th century. An example is the work of Sir William Jones in India (also see Section 3.1).

As modern languages are held to have descended from ancient languages, historical comparative linguistics describes this process of evolution and development as well as the similarities in the process of this language change. The comparative and historical methods are based on discovering relationships between languages. A language (say, L) from which other languages have developed is called a **proto-language**, or a parent language. Languages that develop from it (e.g. L_1, L_2) are in a sense later stages of this proto-language, and these languages L_1, L_2, ... are sister languages. All these taken together form a language family, e.g. an earlier language, called Proto-Indo-European, was the parent language, from which languages such as Latin, Greek, Sanskrit, and German, developed. A simplified chart illustrating this is shown in Fig. 2.1.

Fig. 2.1 Language family.

This proto-language is not something that exists now; it is reconstructed by historical linguists on the basis of written records, coins, inscriptions, and so on. A proto-language can never be reconstructed completely, and it is a complex and laborious task to trace the similarities between languages that enable the reconstruction of the proto-language. However, historical and comparative linguists make lists of words from different languages and compare the sound similarities and the occurrence of sounds in particular position in these words. That is, these linguists look for sound correspondences and build **cognates**. A cognate is a word which is related genetically to other words which together form a set of cognates descended from a proto-language. For example, there is a set of words:

frater (Latin)
brother (English)
bhrata (Sanskrit)

These are cognates belonging to a set relating to a word which may have existed in Proto-Indo-European. In each cognate there is some sound similarity that shows that there is a genetic link; however, there is also a sound change which indicates that each belongs to different languages.

In this way, the comparative linguist attempts to construct cognate sets and attempts to reconstruct proto-forms so as to give an account of the changes that have occurred in the development of languages. Though historical linguistics and comparative linguistics study the laws operating in language change and in the formation and development of languages, this can only be done by describing the related languages. Hence this type of study is related to descriptive linguistics. Also, descriptive linguistics takes account of language change when it studies two or more varieties of a language that exist at a particular time. When two or more descriptions of language are contrasted (e.g. Tamil and Hindi), it is known as **contrastive linguistics**. This is based on synchronic description of the languages, i.e. it is not historical.

The distinction between descriptive (synchronic) and historical (diachronic) linguistics is made by means of a diagram, given in Chapter 3, where the distinction is also explained in detail.

To sum up:

Modern linguistics is mainly **descriptive** because it attempts to describe fully and accurately the structure of a language as it exists at a given time. It is a **synchronic** study of language. It describes systems in a language at all levels of structure: The phonological level or system of sounds, the morphological level or system of word formation, the syntactic level, or level of sentence formation, and the semantic system or level of meaning. This is discussed in detail in Section 2.4.

2.4 LEVELS OF LINGUISTIC ANALYSIS

In studying language which is the subject-matter of linguistics, we mark or sub-divide the area in order to study it in an analytical and systematic way. Language has a hierarchical structure. This means that it is made up of units which are themselves made up of smaller units which are made of still smaller units till we have the smallest indivisible unit, i.e. a single distinguishable sound, called a phoneme. Or we can put it the other way round, and say that single sounds or phonemes combine together to make larger units of sounds. These combine into a larger meaningful unit called a morpheme; morphemes combine to form larger units of words; and words combine to form a large unit or sentence; and several sentences combine or interconnect to make a unified piece of speech or writing, which we call a text or discourse. At each stage (or level), there are certain rules that operate which permit the occurrence and combination of smaller units. So we can say that rules of phonology determine the occurrence and combination of particular phonemes, rules of word-formation cover the behaviour of particular morphemes; rules of sentence-formation determine the combination and positioning of words in a sentence. Each level is a **system** in its own right. It is important to remember that, because of the existence of rules at each level, we can analyse each level **independently** of the other. This means that if we study one level, e.g. phonology or the sound-system, we need not necessarily study another level, say that of sentence-formation. We can study phonology on its own, and syntax on its own. Although these levels are linked in that one is lower in the hierarchy and another is higher in the hierarchy, and the higher level includes the lower, still each level is independent because it has its own rules of operation that can be described, analysed and understood.

We can represent these levels in the following manner, with each level of analysis corresponding to each level of the structure of the language:

Levels of Analysis	*Levels of Structure*
Phonetics and Phonology	**Sounds**
Morphology	**Word Formation**
Syntax	**Sentence Formation**
Semantics	**Meanings**
Discourse	**Connected Sentences**

A careful look at the above representation will show that the levels of language structure are not completely separate from one another. In fact, there are important and vital linkages between the levels. In earlier studies, it was supposed that phonology, the level of sound structure, had no link whatsoever with semantics or the level of meaning structure. Now we know that links between these levels are far more complex than we had earlier thought of. With regard to discourse, we can see that it is made up of all the levels of language working together, while semantics incorporates analysis of meaning at the level of both words (word-meaning) and of sentence-meaning.

However, we can study these links only after we describe and analyse structure at each level separately. Thus **Phonetics** studies language at the level of sounds: How sounds are articulated by the human speech mechanism and received by the auditory mechanism, how sounds can be distinguished and characterised by the manner in which they are produced. **Phonology** studies the combination of sounds into organised units of speech, the formation of syllables and larger units. It describes the sound system of a particular language and the combination and distribution of sounds which occur in that language. Classification is made on the basis of the concept of the phoneme, i.e. a distinctive, contrasted sound unit, e.g. /m/, /g/, /p/. These distinct sounds enter into combination with others. The rules of combination are different for different languages.

Though phonology is considered to be the surface or superficial level of language (since it is concrete and not abstract as in the case of meaning), there are some aspects of it such as tone which contribute to the meaning of an utterance.

Morphology studies the patterns of formation of words by the combination of sounds into minimal distinctive units of meaning called morphemes. A morpheme cannot be broken up because if it is, it will no longer make sense, e.g. a morpheme 'bat' is made up of three sounds: /b/ /æ/ and /t/. This combination makes up the single morpheme 'bat', and if broken up, it will no longer carry the meaning of 'bat'. Words can be made up of single morphemes such as 'bat' or combinations of morphemes, e.g. 'bats' is made up of two morphemes: 'bat' + 's'. Morphology deals with the rules of combination of morphemes to form words, as suffixes or prefixes are attached to single morphemes to form words. It studies the changes that take place in the structure of words, e.g. the morpheme 'take' changes to 'took' and 'taken'. These changes signify a change in tense.

The level of morphology is linked to phonology on the one hand and to semantics on the other. It is clear in the above example of 'take' that the change to 'took' involves a change in one of the sounds in this morpheme. It also involves a change in meaning: 'take' means the action 'take' + time present and 'took' means the action 'take' + time past. So morphological changes often involve changes at the levels of both sound and meaning.

Syntax is the level at which we study how words combine to form phrases, phrases combine to form clauses, and clauses join to make sentences. The study of syntax also involves the description of the rules of positioning of elements in the sentence such as the nouns/noun syntax phrases, verbs/verb phrases, and adverbial phrases. A sentence must be composed of these elements arranged in a particular order. Syntax also attempts to describe how these elements function in the sentence, i.e. what is their role in the sentence. For example, the word 'boy' is a noun. However, in each of the following sentences, it functions in different roles:

(a) The **boy** likes cricket.
(b) The old man loved the **boy**.

In sentence (a), it functions as the subject of the sentence.
In sentence (b), it functions as the object.

A sentence should be both grammatical and meaningful. For example, a sentence like 'Colourless green ideas sleep furiously' is grammatically correct but it is not meaningful. Thus, rules of syntax should be comprehensive enough to explain how sentences are constructed which are both grammatical and meaningful.

Semantics deals with the level of meaning in language. It attempts to analyse the structure of meaning in a language, e.g. how words similar or different are related; it attempts to show these inter-relationships through forming 'categories'. Semantics tries to give an account of both word and sentence meaning, and attempts to analyse and define that which is considered to be abstract. It may be easy to define the meanings of words such as 'tree' but not so easy to define the meanings of words such as 'love' or similar abstract things. This is why semantics is one of the less clearly definable areas of language study.

An extension of the study of meaning or semantics is **pragmatics**. Pragmatics deals with the eontextual aspects of meaning in particular situations. As distinct from the study of sentences, pragmatics considers **utterances,** i.e. those sentences which are actually uttered by speakers of a language.

Discourse is the study of chunks of language which are bigger than a single sentence. At this level, we analyse inter-sentential links that form a connected or **cohesive** text. Cohesion is the relation established in a sentence between it and the sentences preceding and following it, by the use of connectives such as 'and', 'though', 'also', 'but' etc. and by the manner in which reference is made to other parts of the text by devices such as repetition or by use of pronouns, definite articles, etc. By studying the elements of cohesion we can understand how a piece of connected language can have greater meaning that is more than the sum of the individual sentences it contains.

In addition to these levels of linguistic analysis, we also study **Graphology** which is the study of the writing system of a language and the conventions used in representing speech in writing, e.g. the formation of letters. **Lexicology** studies the manner in which lexical items (words) are grouped together as in the compilation of dictionaries.

Linguists differ in their views on what precisely is the **scope** of linguistic studies. Some consider the proper area of linguistics to be confined to the levels of phonology, morphology and syntax. This can be called a **Micro-linguistic** perspective. However, some take a broader, or **macro-linguistic** view which includes the other levels of analysis mentioned above, as well as other aspects of language and its relationship with many areas of human activity.

2.5 BRANCHES OF LINGUISTICS

The **core** of linguistic studies is the study of language structure at different levels as discussed above. In the growth of modern linguistics as an autonomous field of knowledge, it has been necessary to emphasize this aspect of linguistics since no other field of study describes language structure systematically and completely. However, there are many areas of human activity and knowledge in which language plays a part and linguistics is useful in these areas. The study of language in relation to the many areas of knowledge, where it is relevant, has led to the growth of many branches of linguistics. Thus, the scope of linguistics has grown to include these branches.

Like other sciences, linguistics has a 'pure' or 'theoretical' aspect which is concerned with the building of theories about language and with description and analysis of particular levels of language such as phonology and syntax without regard to any particular applications that these may have. It also has an 'applied' aspect which is concerned with the application of that knowledge in areas such as the learning and teaching of languages, or correction and improvement of speech disorders, or in helping us to appreciate the use of language in literature. Thus, 'applied linguistics' covers many of the branches of linguistics that explore the practical application of the theories, concepts and analyses provided by linguists. All the applications are first and foremost based on a thorough description of languages. As Corder (1973, p. 148) writes:

> Whether it is speech therapy, psychiatry, literary criticism, translation,... what all these fields of application have in common is the necessity for descriptions of the various languages involved.

Various branches of linguistics have grown because language is intimately related both to the **inner** world of man's mind and to the **outer** world of society and social relationships. Each of these aspects has led to the study of **psycholinguistics** and **sociolinguistics,** respectively.

2.51 Psycholinguistics

Since language is a mental phenomenon, mental processes are articulated in language behaviour. Psycholinguistics studies these mental processes, processes of thought, and concept formation and their articulation in language, which reveal a great deal about the structures of both human psychology and of language. 'Cognitive' psychology is the area which explores how meanings are understood by the human brain, how syntax and memory are linked, how messages are 'decoded' and stored. Psycholinguistics also studies the influence of psychological factors such as intelligence, motivation, anxiety etc. on the kind of language that is understood and produced. For instance, in the case of errors made by a speaker, there may be psychological reasons which influence comprehension or production that are responsible for the occurrence of an error. Our perception of speech sounds or graphic symbols (in writing) is influenced by the state of our mind. One kind of mental disability, for example, results in the mistakes made by children in reading when they mistake one letter for another (Dyslexia). Psycholinguistics can offer some insights and corrective measures for this condition.

Psycholinguistics is concerned with the learning of language at various stages: the early acquisition of a first language by children and later stages in acquisition of first and other languages. Psycholinguists attempt to answer questions such as whether the human brain has an inborn language ability structured in such a way that certain grammatical and semantic patterns are embedded in it, which can explain how all human beings are capable of learning a language. This exploration may lead us to determining whether all the languages in the world have some 'universal' grammar that lies in the mind of every human being and is transformed in particular situations to produce different languages. Psycholinguistic studies in language acquisition are very useful in the area of language teaching because they help teachers to understand error production and individual differences among learners and thus devise appropriate syllabi and materials for them.

One specialized area within psycholinguistics is neurolinguistics that studies the physiological basis of language and language disorders such as aphasia, loss of memory, etc.

Another relation of language with mind is that of logic. It was held by some ancient philosophers that the human mind is rational and capable of thinking logically and, therefore, language too is logically ordered and rational. Others held that, just as irrationality is present in the mind, irregularity or anomaly is present in human language. Since then there has been a debate about the nature of language and the relation between language and logic. One of the problems discussed by **philosophers of language** is whether language can be an adequate medium for philosophical inquiry. Since all our thoughts are known to us through language, we must examine the kind of language we use when we approach philosophical issues and analysis.

2.52 Sociolinguistics

The branch of linguistics that deals with the exploration of the relation between language and society is known as **sociolinguistics**, and the **sociology of language**. Sociolinguistics is based on the fact that language is not a single homogeneous entity, but has different forms in different situations. The changes in language occur because of changes in social conditions, for example, social class, gender, regional and cultural groups. A particular social group may speak a different variety of a language from the rest of the community. This group becomes a speech community.

Variation in language may occur because the speakers belong to a different geographical region. Taking the example of English, we find that it is not a single language but exists in the form of several varieties. One kind of English is called R.P. (or Received Pronunciation). This kind of English is used in the south west of England and particularly associated with the universities of Oxford and Cambridge and the BBC. It is an educated and formal kind of English. But there are other varieties of English, such as the English that is spoken in the north of England, in Yorkshire and Lancashire; in Scotland (Scottish English); Wales (Welsh English), etc. A less educated variety of English is that spoken by working class people in London often called Cockney English. Then there are the varieties of English spoken by people of different countries around the world, e.g. American English, Indian English and Australian English.

Sociolinguistics is the study of language variation and change—how varieties of language are formed when the speakers belong to a geographical region, social class, social situation and occupation, etc. Varieties of a language that are formed in various geographical regions involve a change in the pronunciation as well as vocabulary. Such changes result in the formation of a distinctly different variety of the language or a **dialect**. Sometimes these changes may be present within the same geographical region due to the social differences between different economic sections, e.g. working class and aristocracy. These changes result in **class-dialects.**

In sociolinguistic studies, we consider the linguistic features of these dialects, e.g. syntax variations such as 'I've **gotten** it' or 'I ain't seen nothing' and lexical variations such as 'lift' (British English) for 'elevator' (American English). The study of the demarcation of dialect boundaries across a region and of specific features of each dialect is called **dialectology**. One dialect may be demarcated from another by listing a number of features which occur in a particular region. The point at which a certain feature (of pronunciation or vocabulary) ceases to be prevalent and gives way to another feature is a dialect boundary or 'isogloss'. Dialects may acquire some importance and prestige and evolve into distinct languages. This usually happens when they are codified, e.g. in written and literary forms, and when their grammar and lexicon are standardized. Usually, this happens when the dialect is given political and social importance. That is why it is said "A language is a dialect with an army, and navy". Sociolinguists chart the evolution of such changes.

Variation in language may also be due to the specific area of human activity in which language is used. Again taking the example of English, this language is used in different fields—of law, religion, science, sports etc. In each of these areas there is a specific vocabulary and manner of use of English, which defines the legal language, the scientific language etc. This variety of language according to its **use**, is called **register**. Sociolinguists examine the particular characteristics of different registers, i.e. legal register, scientific register, etc., to see how these differ. This kind of study is useful because it enables us to understand how language-use is tied to a social context. The notion of register is important in showing that language use in communication is not arbitrary or uncontrolled, but is governed by rules of situational and contextual appropriateness.

The sociology of language includes the study of attitudes to language held by social groups, for instance, they may consider some languages or dialects as more (or less) important. It includes the planning of language education, e.g. which languages should be the medium of instruction, which language should be taught as second language; and language policy, i.e. which languages are legally and constitutionally recognised and what status they are given. The sociology of language is thus linked with other aspects of our social world, the political, economic, educational, etc.

2.53 Anthropological Linguistics

The evolution of language in human society and its role in the formation of culture is another aspect of language, society and culture. This is studied in **anthropological linguistics**. The structure of language has a social and cultural basis in the same way as other customs, conventions and codes such as those related to dress and food. Each culture organises its world in its own way, giving names to objects, identifying areas of significance or value and suppressing other areas. Language becomes a way of embodying the world view and beliefs of a culture, and the things that culture holds sacred; for example, a culture in which family relationships occupy the most significant position will have many kinship terms in their language, with each relationship specified by a particular term. If you compare the kinship terms in English such as grandfather, grandmother, uncle, aunt, etc. with kinship terms in Hindi, you will find that there are many more such terms in Hindi specifying particular relationships such as a paternal/maternal grandfather (ḍa : ḍa/na : na) and many such terms that specify the relationships elaborately.

Similarly, terms specifying colours, emotions, natural phenomena, and so on are differently organised in every culture, and reveal a great deal about that culture. The study of these specific cultural elements is called the **ethnography** of a culture. A specific way of communication in a culture is thus studied as the ethnography of communication.

Anthropological studies have explored the relation between language and culture. Language is invented to communicate and express a culture. It also happens that this language then begins to determine the way we think and see the world. Since this language is the means by which we understand and think about the world, we cannot go beyond it and understand the world in any other way. This is the view expressed by the linguist B.L. Whorf whose hypothesis is that we dissect nature along the lines laid by our native language. There is still a debate about this, but it is true that to some extent we are bound to see the world according to the terms specified by our own language. These aspects of language and culture are still being discussed by anthropological linguists, philosophers of language and ethnographers.

2.54 Literary Stylistics

The study of variation in language and the use of language in communication has also led to new ways of studying literary texts and the nature of literary communication. If you consider again the notion of register discussed above, you may realise that register is in fact a kind of 'language' that is considered appropriate for a particular subject matter, e.g. the style of a religious sermon, the style of sports commentary. Similarly we may use this notion to describe the style of a literary work. That is, we may describe its features at the levels of phonology, syntax, lexis, etc. to distinguish it from other texts and to appreciate how it achieves some unique effects through the use of language. This kind of study is called **literary stylistics**.

Literary writers use the system of language in their own way, i.e. they create a style. This is done by deliberate **choice** (e.g. out of a whole range of words available, they choose one which would be particularly effective), sometimes by **deviation** from or violation of the rules of grammar (e.g. 'he danced his did' in Cummings' poem). Poets and even prose writers may invert the normal order of items in a sentence (e.g. 'Home is the sailor...') or create a pattern by **repetition** of some items (e.g. the sound /f/ in 'the furrow followed free'). By these and other devices, they are able to manipulate language so that it conveys some theme or meaning with great force and effectiveness.

In literary stylistics, we read the text closely with attention to the features of language used in it, identifying and listing the particular features under the heading of 'lexis', 'grammar', 'phonology' or 'sound patterns'. When we have obtained a detailed account of all these features, we co-relate them or bring them together in an interpretation of the text. That is, we try to link '**what** is being said' with '**how** it is being said,' since it is through the latter that writers can fully express the many complex ideas and feelings that they want to convey. Stylistic analysis also helps in a better understanding of how metaphor, irony, paradox, ambiguity etc. operate in a literary text as these are all effects achieved through language and through the building up of a coherent linguistic structure.

2.55 Relationship between Branches of Linguistics

We can understand the extension of the scope of linguistics to its various branches with the help of Fig. 2.2, which also helps us to see the interconnection between these different and yet interrelated areas of study.

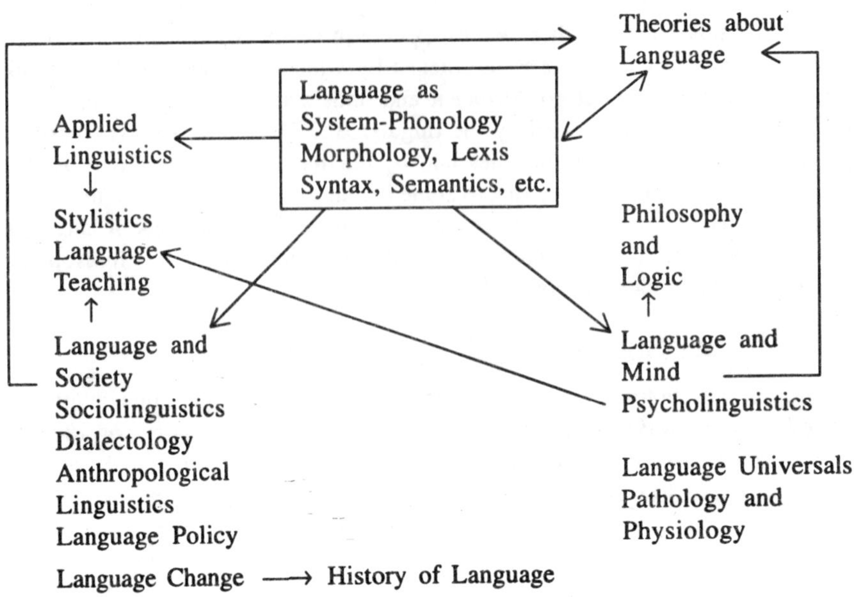

Fig. 2.2 Branches of linguistics.

Language as a system described at all levels is at the centre of the diagram. It relates on one side to man's outer world, i.e. the social, cultural, educational, and literary aspects of use of language in this world, on the other side to man's inner world, i.e. psychological and mental processes and activities, thought and logic. The arrows indicate the inter-relationships between all these areas (This diagram is a modification from Halliday, 1978; p. 16).

SUMMARY

Linguistics is defined as the scientific study of language.

Linguistics is a science in that

(i) it is empirical and objective;
(ii) its explanation of language is based on observation of language phenomena; and
(iii) its explanations are consistent and economical.

The concern of linguistics (its scope) is (a) to describe language, (b) to study the nature of language, and (c) to establish a theory of language.

In undertaking language study, linguists follow several approaches:

1. Descriptive approach which means describing the structure of language.
2. Comparative approach which entails comparing languages and establish correspondences between them.
3. Historical approach which involves examining the history and evolution of languages.

The levels of linguistic analysis, corresponding to the levels of language structure, are: Phonetics and phonology, morphology, syntax, semantics, which take sounds, words, sentences, and meanings, respectively as discrete units. Discourse is the level of language beyond the sentence.

As modern linguistics has developed, it has grown from an autonomous discipline to one linked with various other disciplines such as psychology, sociology, philosophy, literary studies, etc. Thus, many branches of linguistics have developed, such as sociolinguistics, psycholinguistics, language pathology, anthropological linguistics, dialectology, literary stylistics, and so on. Research in all these areas has facilitated the application of insights from linguistics in language teaching and planning of language education and policies.

COMPREHENSION QUESTIONS

1. What is the particular way in which linguists approach language as opposed to a layman's view of language?
2. What is the difference between a linguist and a polyglot?
3. What scientific procedures do linguists employ in the study of language?
4. Define:

   (a) Descriptive linguistics
   (b) Historical linguistics
   (c) Comparative linguistics

   Do you find any inter-relationship between these approaches to the study of language?
5. How is linguistics an autonomous discipline?
6. Illustrate how we describe language at different levels of hierarchical organisation.
7. How are different linguistic levels linked to each other?
8. Why are there several branches of linguistics and what are they?
9. How does the study of sociolinguistics help us in understanding language? What aspects of language are emphasized by this branch of linguistics?

CHAPTER 3

Some Fundamental Concepts and Distinctions in Linguistics

3.1 BACKGROUND

Modern linguistics is based on some fundamental concepts which were expounded by linguists in the beginning of the twentieth century. The most influential of these were:

(i) The representatives of the American School of structural anthropologists, chiefly Leonard Bloomfield; and after World War II, the work of Noam Chomsky.

(ii) The European linguists, chiefly among them the Swiss linguist Ferdinand de Saussure.

The main ideas regarding language propounded by these linguists take the form of certain **distinctions** or **dichotomies** by means of which we have been able to understand the nature of language in a more systematic and complete way. Some of the basic distinctions, dichotomies and concepts are discussed now:

3.2 THE LANGUE/PAROLE DISTINCTION, AND COMPETENCE VERSUS PERFORMANCE

Saussure made a distinction between two aspects of language: **Langue** and **Parole**. **Langue** means language, that is, all the rules and conventions regarding the combinations of sounds, formation of words and sentences, pronunciation and meaning. All these conventions constitute **langue** and are a product of social agreement. That is, there is a similarity of sounds, words and meaning among the native speakers of a language which means that they have the same images and signs in their minds. As Saussure (1916) puts it:

> If we embrace the sum of word-images stored in the mind of all individuals we could identify the social bond that constitutes language. It is a storehouse filled by the members of a given community through their active use, a grammatical system that has a potential existence in each brain, or more specifically, in the brains of a group of individuals.

> For language is not complete in any speaker; it exists perfectly only within a collectivity.

This means that:

(i) **Langue** is **social**, a set of conventions shared by all the speakers of a language.

(ii) **Langue** is **abstract**, as these particular conventions exist in the minds of the speakers who belong to that society that has created the language.

Parole, on the other hand, belongs to the individual. When those conventions that exist in the mind as **langue** are used in a concrete form in actual speech or writing, they become instances of **parole. Parole** is the actual sounds and sentences produced by an individual speaker or writer. It is a concrete physical manifestation of the abstract **langue** that exists in the mind. If we hear a person speaking a language that we do not know, we hear the sounds and sentences, that is, the **parole**, but we cannot understand them because we do not share the conventions or **langue** that are behind the individual sounds and sentences. So **langue** is the underlying system which makes the individual performance or **parole** meaningful. Without it, **parole** would never be understood and could not serve as a means of communication.

Thus, **parole** is:

(i) **Individual** performance of language in speech or writing.

(ii) **Concrete** and physical. It makes use of the physiological mechanism such as speech organs, in uttering words and sentences.

Thus, **langue** exists in the mind of each individual in the form of word-images and knowledge of conventions, that is, as an abstract form of the grammar and dictionary of the language. An individual makes use of this knowledge, in his or her own way to produce actual sentences, i.e. **parole**. Individuals can communicate with each other because they share the same **langue**, but they produce different sentences based on the same **langue**. Their production of sentences (**parole**) is marked as being variable, unpredictable, heterogeneous, inventive and whimsical, but even then, it has to follow the stable conventions of **langue** if it has to communicate. It can be said that the language system is **langue** while **language behaviour** is **parole**.

Saussure (1916) considered **langue** as the **legislative** side of language or the law of the language. Like law, langue maintains the social order and homogeneity of the language, and is relatively fixed, i.e. it does not change with each individual. **Parole** is the **executive** side of the language because it uses the law or code of the language (i.e. **langue**) for its individual ends. It executes **langue** through individual acts of speaking and writing.

Another useful comparison between langue and **parole** is made by the analogy of a game of chess. In the game, the rules are determined and they are understood by all the players, but each game is different and depends on the individual performances which differ from player to player.

According to Saussure, we can only study **langue** and not **parole**, because **langue** is a well-defined, homogenous object distinct from the heterogeneous, unpredictable mass of speech acts. **Langue** consists of signs which bear the stamp of collective approval and which exist as psychological associations having their seat in the brain. These signs can be converted into conventional written symbols, so they can be studied. Individual acts of speaking, on the other hand, cannot be accurately represented, and are so variable that they cannot be studied. Therefore, only **langue** and not **parole** is the fit object for study.

This concept is also explained by the American linguist Noam Chomsky who made a similar distinction between **competence** and **performance**. Competence, according to Chomsky, is the native speaker's knowledge of his language, the mastery of the system of rules, while performance is the production of actual sentences in use in real-life situations. So a speaker's knowledge of the structure of the language is the speaker's **linguistic competence**, and the way in which he uses it is **linguistic performance**. While competence is a set of principles which a speaker masters, performance is what a speaker does. The former is a kind of code, the latter is the act of encoding or decoding. In other words, the abstract or the internal grammar which enables a speaker to utter and understand an infinite number of potential utterances is a speaker's competence. Competence is free from interference due to slips of memory, lapses of attention, etc., while performance reflects many such lapses. Therefore competence is ideal, and as it gives us a coherent picture of the language, it is competence that can be studied, whereas it is difficult to get a direct, coherent record of performance.

This understanding of competence vs performance as given by Chomsky closely resembles the **langue/parole** dichotomy given by Saussure. But it differs in that while **langue** is the same with every language user, competence may differ from person to person. Saussure's understanding of **langue** emphasises its predominantly social aspect, while Chomsky's term 'competence' is based on psychology and presumes individual differences between human beings. Thus speaker A may be more competent than B, though they may share the same conventions of language. Similarly A's performance would also be different from that of B. Chomsky's view of competence is also based on the idea of an inbuilt language acquisition device in humans that enables a person to acquire competence, i.e. to internalize the system of the rules of the language, enabling him to generate an infinite number of sentences.

In recent years, there has been some argument about these distinctions. Some sociolinguists regard these dichotomies as unreal. **Langue** and **parole** are inter-related and not separate. Just as **parole** is not possible or effective without **langue**, **langue** also changes gradually under the effect of **parole**. Saussure (1916) himself says: "Speech has both an individual and a social side, and we cannot conceive of one without the other". But the sociolinguists' objection is that **parole** can also be studied as it is concerned with the use of language in social situations which ultimately do have an effect on **langue**. We cannot keep **parole**, or performance out of our study of language because it also gives us useful insight into language-processes and it also has some features which are systematic and predictable in given social situations. Moreover, it is now easier to study performance through recording by audio and video devices. It is, after all, through the study of performance or **parole** that we can obtain the data that gives us a better understanding of **langue or competence.**

However, the distinction is still useful, as it enables us to understand the two aspects of language and to study each of them in a more systematic manner.

3.3 THE NATURE OF THE LINGUISTIC SIGN AND SIGN/SYMBOL DISTINCTION

The language system is made up of signs. In fact, as Saussure says, sign is the central fact of language. What is the sign and what is its nature?

A sign is a physical marker which carries some information. The information it gives is direct, brief and precise (meaning only this, no other). This is opposed to symbol which means more than mere indication. It contains more information and stands in place of something as a means of pointing towards it indirectly. For example, the gesture of waving one's hand is a sign, but can be interpreted variously as symbolic of farewell, dismissal etc. Similarly, a way of dressing or eating is a sign which signals some social practice or belief. This concept, when applied to all our behaviour and to our society and culture, shows us that our entire culture is made up of signs which are of special significance or meaning in our culture. Saussure's notion of sign in this sense has led to the growth of a whole area of study of the operation of signs in culture and society, called **Semiotics.**

In language studies too, this helps us to understand what language is. The linguistic sign consists of two parts. The **signifier** and the **signified** or the word which signifies and the object that is signified as

Signifies
Tree ————→ 

But the word 'tree' does not signify the actual object that is, the tree. If it did, the word for this object in all languages would have been the same, i.e. 'tree'. But we know that this object is called by different names in different languages. This means that the word 'tree' does not represent the actual object in real life. It represents the concept or the image of the object that we have in our minds. We see an object in the real world and form a concept of it in our minds. We invent a word consisting of some sound-images which we then use to represent the concept that exists in our minds. There is no logical reason why we choose a certain combination of sounds to represent the concept. So we say that the relationship between the sounds (& words) and the concept they signify is an arbitrary one.

Let us therefore modify the earlier diagram regarding sign in the following manner:

Tree ————→ Signifies ————→ Concept of tree
(word or sound image = signifier) (mental image = signified)

That which signifies (the 'word') is the signifier. That which is signified (the 'concept') is the signified. Sign is the composite of both, i.e. it consists of the relationship between the signifier and the signified. This relationship, once established, continues over a long period of time. It is established as a social fact, i.e. by society, since it is an arbitrary, not a logical, relationship. That is, as it is not established by reason (there is no inherent, reasonable connection between the object and the sounds used to represent it), only social agreement can give it validity. It becomes valid and acceptable, therefore, only through social agreement. There is no intrinsic basis to it. This is how the linguistic sign is arbitrary.

Many such signs make up the system of a language. Signs are **relational entities**, they exist only in terms of relation to each other. They enter into complex relationships with each other and these relationships constitute the whole system of the language. Since signs are based on arbitrary relationships, they differ from one language to another. Concepts about the signified (i.e. 'object') differ from one language to another. Every society constructs its own concepts of the real world and links these concepts to certain signifiers and signifieds arbitrarily chosen in any way it wants. But once the relationships are made, individuals are not free to choose any arbitrary signifiers they want to choose.

A symbol is a kind of sign that signifies several concepts on the basis of the primary relationship between signifier and signified. That is, the word 'tree' signifies the concept of tree—this is the primary relationship. It may also signify 'life', 'growth', etc., and when it does, it becomes not only a sign but also a symbol. So a symbol is built up of several associative relationships between the signifiers and the signifieds. That is why we say that language is a system of symbolic signs since there are often very complex associative relationships between the signifiers and the signifieds in a language.

3.4 THE STRUCTURE/SYSTEM DISTINCTION, SYNTAGMATIC AND PARADIGMATIC RELATIONSHIPS

We say that language is **structured** and that it is **a system of systems**. This means that it is structured in such a way that its elements are inter-related to form a system at each level of its structure. Thus, sounds are inter-related to form the phonological system, words are inter-related to form the morphological system, and word-classes are inter-related to form the syntactic system.

To give an example of this, Robins compares the structure of language to that of an orchestra. The members of an orchestra are all related to each other by their specific roles as orchestra players in the orchestra as a whole, and as smaller groups within the orchestra (e.g. group of violinists, group of bass players). Each performs his function by virtue of his place in relation to the others and players cannot be added to or taken away from an orchestra without changing its quality. This is what we mean by structure: an ordered composition of many parts, each part being related to the whole, and also related to other elements within it. Each part, by inter-relationship of elements in it, constitutes a system.

Within each system, elements are selected and **combined** in building up the structure. For example, if we wish to build up a word such as 'take', we will select some sounds—out of several sounds possible, we select /t/, /eɪ/ and /k/, and then we combine them in a particular order, i.e. we decide which one is to occur first, and which later. In the process of selection, certain rules operate: we can select one element at a time from among a class of similar elements, e.g. a particular consonant from a class of similar consonants; a noun from a class of nouns. With reference to the above example, we chose the consonant /t/ instead of /k/ or /b/, and so on, which we could have chosen because they are all similar, i.e. they are all plosives. They belong to the same category of sounds. The relationship between those elements which are similar because they belong to the same class or category is called a **paradigmatic relationship** which holds between several elements that belong to the same class within a system, e.g. the relationship between plosive consonants in the phonological system, or the relationship between nouns in the syntactic system.

In the process of combination of these elements we combine the chosen elements in a particular order or sequence. Here, too, there are certain rules. For instance, we can combine /t/ + /eɪ/ + /k/ in this order, but not in the order: /eɪ/ + /t/ + /k/. It is obvious that there is a particular order or **sequence** which must be followed. The three elements that follow one another in a particular sequence are related in what can be called a **syntagmatic relationship**. One follows the other in a linear order, and it is by following this order that the structure of a word or sentence is built up. Thus,

Paradigmatic relationship = between elements in a class or system, only one can operate at a time.

Syntagmatic relationship = between elements in a linear sequence, structural

Or to illustrate with an example:

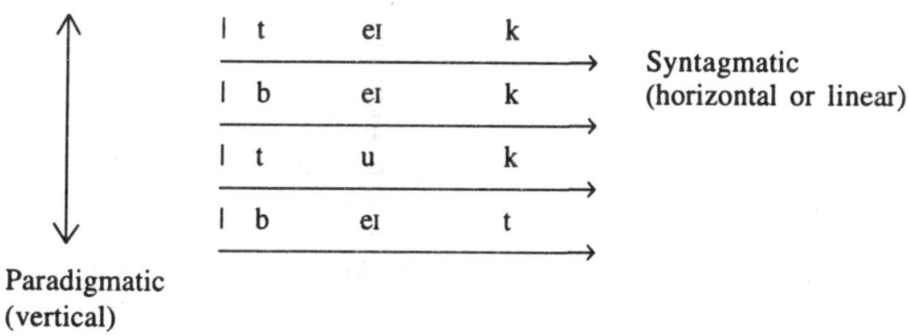

In the paradigmatic relationship, /t/ can be replaced by /b/, /eɪ/ can be replaced by /u/, /k/ can be replaced by /t/. Each can be replaced by another element from within the same system and class. So, in the above example, we cannot put a consonant in place of the vowel but we can replace one vowel by another. In the syntagmatic relationship, the elements have to be combined in the proper sequence. We cannot violate the sequential order. On the basis of these paradigmatic and systagmatic relationships, rules of selection and combination operate, and taken together, these constitute the structure of a language. They are like the two intersecting threads that build up the fabric of language. Because of these relationships we say that language has duality of structure. At one level, we select particular elements out of many, at another level, we combine these elements to form a structural unit. With a limited number of elements we can construct a large number of combinations. In the example given below, we see how both selection (paradigmatic) and combination (syntagmatic) processes enable us to construct different sentences:

The	boy	went	to school
A	boy	went	to school
The	boy	went	home
The	boy	ran	home
The	girl	went	to school
A	girl	ran	home

Other variations are also possible, depending on what elements are chosen from each category at the paradigmatic level. Each category has elements which are discrete and separable from elements in another category and, therefore, elements in each category are able to operate independently as representatives, as it were, of that whole category. This gives us a lot of flexibility, or choice of the elements which we wish to combine. At the syntagmatic level too, variations are possible, but there are rules which allow for only certain kinds of variation. For example in the above sentence, the rules of sequentiality (syntagmatic) allow us to substitute 'home' for 'to school' because both these can function in the adjunct position at the end of the sentence; but we cannot have 'To school the boy went' or 'Went home the girl', because these violate the syntagmatic relationship between the elements (Sometimes poets violate this relationship, e.g. 'Home is the sailor, Home from the sea/And the hunter Home from the hill'—this is done for the sake of emphasis and to create a particular rhythm).

To sum up, system is the set of paradigmatic relationships between elements, and structure is the set of syntagmatic relationships between elements at each level in the language. At the level of sounds, there is a phonological system (consisting, for instance, of vowels and consonants) and a **phonological structure** (determining the combination of these vowels and consonants). At the level of sentence-formation, there is a **syntactic system** (consisting of word-classes such as noun, verb, adjective, adverb) and a **syntactic structure** (determining the combination of these word-classes) to enable the formation of sentences.

3.5 SUBSTANCE AND FORM

Sounds and symbols such as letters of the alphabet that represent sounds in writing are the raw material of a language. They are the phonic (sound) and graphic (written) **substance** of the language. In themselves, they have no meaning. It is only when they are given a particular shape or order that they become meaningful. That is, it is only when they have some **form** that they have meaning.

All distinct sounds produced by human speech organs and written scripts are the substance of human language. A cluster of sounds such as /n/, /t/, /e/ etc. is only noise, it has no meaning; it must be suitably arranged into some form to make it meaningful. It is only when the sounds are arranged in a certain way, i.e. /n/ + /e/ + /t/ that we can see some meaning in them. It is just as if there is a log of wood which has no particular shape, and the carpenter makes a chair or table out of it—he has changed the substance into form.

Substance and form are two parts of the quality of language. Substance, which is the mere sound or word is only the 'signifier' in Saussure's terms, and in order to make sense it has to be linked with the 'signified' that is, the meaning, or the concept. Sounds when arranged in a particular order, signify something meaningful; words when arranged in a particular order express some meaningful idea or action; this means that the arrangement itself gives form to the substance of the language. This is why Saussure emphasises the **syntagmatic or associative** arrangement in language.

There is a further distinction to be made between levels of 'expression' and 'content' in form. At one level, the level of expression, linguistics deals with the form or shape of linguistic elements, without necessarily taking into account their meaning. By arranging elements with regard to this level alone, we can get sentences like: 'The bachelor gave birth to a baby' which does not make any sense. So we have to consider the level of content as well, that is, the level of meaning, or semantics. In other words, form includes both grammar (the arrangement of words in the sentence) and semantics (the meaningful relationships between the words).

To sum up, we can say that substance is the elements or 'raw materials' of language such as phonemes, morphemes, or graphemes, and form is the associative order in which these are brought together in a meaningful way. Linguists therefore emphasise that form is the concern of linguistic study, not substance; and it is **form** that makes it possible to study substance.

3.6 DIACHRONIC AND SYNCHRONIC APPROACHES

This distinction is made in linguistics between two approaches to the study of language. The synchronic ('Chronos' stands for 'time') approach sees language as a living whole, existing as a 'state' at one particular time. This 'state' of language is an accumulation of all the linguistic activities that a language community engages in during a specific period. To study language, therefore, linguistics can collect samples of this language as it exists, describing them regardless of any historical considerations which may have influenced the language at any previous time. Once linguists have isolated a focal point for synchronic description, the time factor becomes irrelevant. Whatever changes are taking place in the material as they study it, are considered irrelevant to the main focus of study—which is the system of the language as it exists, that is, the system of inter-relationships that bind together co-existing items in the collective mind of the community.

The diachronic approach, on the other hand 'traces the historical development of the language and records the changes that have taken place in it between successive points in time; 'diachronic' is therefore equivalent to 'historical' (Lyons, 1983, p. 35). It investigates language changes as they have occurred from time to time, and the evolution of languages.

Saussure (1916), who made this distinction, gives priority in linguistics to the synchronic approach, and observes that the two approaches must be kept separate. This is because, as he states, what strikes us first when we study the facts of language is that their succession in time does not exist as far as the speaker is concerned. For instance, a speaker of English is not concerned with the language as it existed in the middle ages. The speaker is confronted with a state of being that is the language as it exists for him at a given time.

Saussure has given the inter-relationship of diachrony and synchrony in this way:

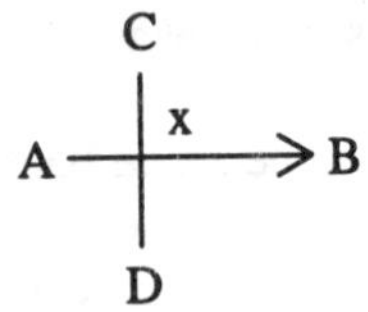

In the diagram, AB is the synchronic axis of simultaneities, i.e. all the facts of language as they co-exist at a particular time. It is the static axis. CD is the **diachronic axis of successions**. That is, CD is an imaginary line moving through time, the historical path through which language has travelled and will continue travelling. AB can intersect CD at any point because at any given time, there will be a number of simultaneous facts about the language co-existing. X is the point on CD where the particular point in time can be isolated and the language as it exists at that point can be described.

The priority of synchronic over diachronic study is explained by Saussure by analogy with the game of chess. The chessboard is constantly changing during the game, as each player makes his move. But if someone walks into the room at any moment during the game, he can understand the state of the game by looking at the positions occupied by the pieces. It does not matter how many moves or what kind of moves have been made before arriving at that stage in the game, the game can be described without reference to the earlier moves. In the same way, Saussure says, as the respective value of the pieces depends on their position on the chessboard, each linguistic term derives its value from its opposition to all the other terms. The rules that are agreed upon before the game begins continue to operate with each move. Similar rules exist in language too. To pass from one stage to the next, only one piece needs to be moved at a time. Thus in language, change effects only isolated elements, not the whole language. Of course, these changes ultimately do result in changing the language, just as a succession of moves can change the outcome of the game. However, at each point in the game all the pieces exist relative to each other and we cannot say what their ultimate fate will be at that point.

Therefore, language can and should be described synchronically, on its own terms without reference to what it has developed from or what it is likely to develop into. However, this does not mean that diachronic or historical study cannot be done. Even Saussure says that though the diachronic perspective is not related to the language system it does affect or condition the system. His attempt is only to keep the two apart because language is a complex system of values and we may confuse synchronic description if we take the historical perspective into account while doing so. Also, to give historical studies a better and more valid base, good synchronic study is essential. We will understand better how these perspectives in linguistics have developed by tracing the history of linguistics in the next chapter.

SUMMARY

Some important concepts and distinctions in language lie at the basis of language study. These are:

1. **Langue** and **parole**, and between competence and performance. **Langue** is the underlying system of rules in the language, conventionally accepted, fixed and abstract in nature. **Parole** is the individual, variable and concrete aspect of language. Competence is the intuitive mastery of the rules of a language by the native speakers of that language, while performance is the actual speech and utterances of the speakers, which are infinite and variable.
2. **Sign** and **symbol**: Sign is made up of signifier and signified taken together. A symbol is based on concepts and associative relationships between signifier and signified.
3. **Structure** and **system**: Structure is an ordered construct, containing many parts within it. Each set of inter-relationships between the parts becomes a system.
4. **Substance** and **form**: The actual sounds and graphic symbols are the substance of language. When they are arranged in order, they attain form.
5. **Syntagmatic** and **paradigmatic** relationships: The former are sequential relationships between elements, the latter are class relationships between elements belonging to the same class.
6. **Synchronic** and **diachronic** approach: The former approaches language in regard to its state at a given time and describes it as it exists. The latter approaches language historically.

COMPREHENSION QUESTIONS

1. Mark the following statements as true or false:
   (a) **Langue** changes, but **parole** doesn't.

(b) The relation between signifier and signified is arbitrary.
(c) Diachronic studies do not take the historical evolution of language into account.
(d) The syntagmatic relationship exists on a horizontal plane.

2. Why is it necessary to distinguish between **langue** and **parole**? Why does Saussure say that langue is the legislative part of language and **parole** is the executive part?

CHAPTER 4

Modern Linguistics: A Historical Survey

4.1 THE BACKGROUND

The study of language is almost as old as language and civilization, though the growth of the modern science of linguistics as we know it now is fairly recent. There is discussion on the importance and origin of language in many ancient religious texts including the Bible and the Vedas. Language was studied on a systematic basis in ancient India and in ancient Greece and Rome. These studies established the foundation for subsequent developments. Some of the ideas and methods of these traditional schools are discussed briefly below, as this will help us understand the growth of modern linguistics and the work and contribution of thinkers such as Bloomfield and Saussure.

4.2 THE INDIAN TRADITION

The religious hymns of the Hindus were composed in Sanskrit around 1800–1200 BC. Sanskrit became the language of religion, of 'mantra' and of ritual. There was a belief that this language should be preserved in its original grammar and pronunciation for the effective practice of religious rituals. Sanskrit grammar originated as an attempt to preserve the classical language of the scriptures. This led to a comprehensive description of Sanskrit at the levels of phonetics, grammar and semantics. Thus a tradition of scholarship in linguistics developed which spanned several centuries.

The most important name in Sanskrit linguistics is that of the grammarian Panini (around 400 BC), who gave a detailed description of Sanskrit grammar. Bloomfield (1933, p.11) wrote about Panini's grammar that it is "one of the greatest monuments of human intelligence. It describes, in minute detail, every inflection, derivation and composition, and every syntactic usage of its author's speech. No other language to this day has been so perfectly described". This grammar was discovered by Europeans in the eighteenth century, and it greatly influenced the European scholars. It opened up a new phase in linguistics—that of the comparative study of languages. In 1786, Sir William Jones addressed the Royal Asiatic Society in Calcutta, where he established that Sanskrit was historically related to Latin, Greek and the Germanic languages:

> The Sanskrit language... is of wonderful structure, more perfect than the Greek, more copious than the Latin, and more exquisitely refined than either, yet bearing to both of them a stronger affinity, both in the roots of verbs and in the forms of grammar, than could have been produced by accident; so strong that no philologist could examine Sanskrit, Greek and Latin without believing them to have sprung from some common source, which perhaps, no longer exists... .

The first Sanskrit grammar in English was published early in the nineteenth century, and from 1800 onwards, classical Sanskrit literature was translated into European languages.

Panini's grammar is known as the *Astadhyayi* or Eight Books. It is divided into eight sections and deals chiefly with grammar, though the levels of sound and meaning are also integrated into the study. Some of its features are as follows:

1. Statement of the rules of word formation. These rules, also called 'Sutras' or threads, are in the form of short statements of the processes of word formation. There are statements of the minimal grammatical structures of classes of words such as nouns and verbs, e.g. a noun may have the structure: root + stem + inflectional suffix, as in 'bhajan' where 'bhaj-' is the root and '-an' is the inflectional suffix. Panini gave the idea of an abstract basic form, which is known today as 'morpheme', which by rules of change is converted into actual words. There are rules regarding changes which occur in words at levels of phonology and morphology which are called morphophonemic changes. One of these is the **Sandhi** by which words are joined and compound words obtained. Different types of word compounding were studied and classified.
2. The verb was taken as the core of the sentence and other words were studied in relation to the verb, e.g. the relation of noun to verb was designated as 'Karaka' referring to the action and the agent of action.
3. The concept of zero-representation was explained first by Panini, where an element changes a word but the change is not marked by change in the external form of the word, e.g. in English, the word for plural noun 'sheep' remains the same: sheep + O = sheep. This is a zero component.
4. The theory of sentence structure, which held that words constituting the sentence must belong to appropriate grammatical classes in proper constructions, they must be semantically appropriate with respect to each other and they must be positioned appropriately.

Panini's grammar was very complex and yet economical (concise), and many commentaries have been written to explicate it. One of the great commentaries on Panini is *Mahabhasya* by Patanjali (around 150 BC). Patanjali was also a great phonetician, who, along with other Sanskrit phoneticians and grammarians, described the sounds of Sanskrit and linked phonetics with grammar. Patanjali gave a phonetic description of distinctive sounds and their allophonic variations according to the theory of 'dhvani' and 'sphota' ('dhvani' is the concrete sound, 'sphota' is the abstract underlying form). A sound unit is the 'varna sphota'.

Phonetic description included the process of articulation, the phonetic segments (consonants and vowels) and their synthesis. Further, Patanjali and other phoneticians gave an account of the difference between voiced and voiceless sounds. Features such as pitch, vowel length, syllable quality and tempo were described in detail. The concept of **Sandhi** which is now a widely used one in phonetics, was explained to show the process of joining of words into sequences through phonological assimilation.

There was also a great deal of discussion on problems of semantics, i.e. of word and sentence meaning. Some scholars gave importance to words as independent meaningful units; others considered that words had no independent existence outside the sentence and therefore the sentence comprises a total meaning unit. The latter view was held by Bhartrhari, the author of *Vakyapadhiya* (around 700 AD) who analysed the sentence as an undivided utterance, and also considered metaphorical uses of language. Sanskrit poetics put forward theories and analyses of literary texts. An example is Anandavardhana's theory of poetic language in **Dhvanyaloka** (circa 900 AD).

All these works, especially of Panini and Patanjali, had far-reaching effects on Western linguists and helped to establish a basis for the synchronic description of language and for comparative linguistics.

4.3 THE GREEK AND THE ROMAN TRADITIONS

The Greeks studied language systematically, as they did other areas of human knowledge, and attempted to give philosophical and logical explanations of language. From the very beginning of Greek scholarship, there was a debate on language. Plato's *Cratylus* (427–347 BC) was concerned with the origins of words (etymology) and gave rise to a controversy between **Analogists**, who believed that language was regular and based on logic (Plato was an analogist) and the **Anomalists**, who believed that properties of things were not related to the words used to name them, and that there was a great deal of irregular change taking place in words (this viewpoint was held by the Stoics, a school of philosophers in Greece).

Apart from this philosophical debate, the Greeks gave attention to the areas of etymology, phonetics and grammar. The most well known Greek grammarians were Dionysuis Thrax (100 BC), the author of *Techne,* and Apollonius (200 AD), besides others. Their studies were based on the written language (Greek); on this basis, they classified elements of grammar and gave explanatory rules and definitions which are still regarded as standard. Some of these are:

1. Definition and analysis of the parts of speech, or word-classes. Words as single linguistic units were classified into eight types by Thrax: nouns, verbs, participles, articles, pronouns, prepositions, adverbs and conjunctions. These were further distinguished as the inflected (word-classes in which change occurs, such as noun and verbs) and uninflected (in which there is no variation, e.g. articles, prepositions). Thrax also dealt with description of gender and case in nouns, and tenses in verbs.
2. The sentence was regarded as the upper limit of description and defined as "expressing a complete thought". In the sentence, the nominal (related to

noun) and verbal (related to verb) constituents were considered as most fundamental. Apollonius described Greek sentence structure on the basis of the relationship between noun and verb to each other and the remaining word classes in relation to these two elements. The function of noun and verb constituents was analysed, to yield the distinction between subject and predicate. Apollonius also described constituent structure (i.e. the relation of constituents to each other as parts of sentence structure).

3. Ancient Greek phoneticians were occupied with defining the phonetic values of the Greek alphabet, and with isolating distinctive speech sounds as the primary elements in speech. According to them, a letter has three aspects: its phonetic value (e.g. /a/), its written shape (a), and its name (alpha). (In English, the difference would be that between the sound /æ/, written (a) and name 'ay', sound /b/, letter 'b', name 'bee'.) Thrax identified the main consonants in Greek. Before him, the Stoics had studied the syllable structure of Greek, and permissible sound sequences.

The Greeks evolved a formal terminology for the description of the Greek language that was subsequently adapted in Latin and has continued to be used in grammar. In the Roman times, it was the study of Latin as a classical language (in many ways similar to Sanskrit) which received attention, and grammatical description was based on classical Latin texts. This grammar, which was a refining of the Greek grammars, still serves as a model for the description of other languages.

Chief among the Latin grammarians were Donatus (400 AD) and Priscian (500 AD). They described Latin on the basis of classical literature, e.g. the works of Virgil, Horace and others. Before them, Varro (20 BC) had made etymological and morphological studies in which he reconciled the analogist/anomalist oppositions. According to his account of word-formation, there are regularities but variation is possible. This may be the idea that led to the development of the later concept of **langue** and **parole**. The main areas emphasised by the Latin grammarians are:

1. Refinement of definitions of word classes. Each class was defined with examples from classical texts, and a recognition of interjection as a separate category was made. Like the definitions given by the Greek grammarian Thrax, these definitions are based on the semantic content or quality, e.g. 'a noun indicates an object or thing' 'a verb indicates an action'.
2. Morphological description was made by setting up base forms, e.g. in the case of nouns it is the nominative, singular form of the noun which is the base; in the case of verbs, it is the first person, singular, present, active form of the verb which is the base. 'Aspect' in the verb is also discussed; as well as active/passive and transitive/intransitive distinctions.
3. The main types of sentences defined earlier by the Greek grammarians were described, particular reference was made to the role of relative pronouns in subordinate clauses.

The several thousand manuscripts on the Latin grammar of Priscian and other grammarians represent the unity of Graeco-Roman scholarship on language.

4.4 AFTER THE RENAISSANCE

The European Renaissance, which occurred after the 'Dark Ages' of the medieval period spanning several centuries, recovered some of the learning of the classical thinkers of Greece and Rome. With this, there was a resurgence of interest in languages. As a period of geographical exploration set in, there grew an awareness of other linguistic traditions such as the Hebrew and the Chinese. During the seventeenth century, interest arose in modern European languages with an emphasis on French as a language of elegance and beauty, leading to the establishment of the Port Royal School of Grammar. This school expounded a general theory of grammar based on logic through the medium of languages such as Latin and French. During this time too, English grammars were written. They were preceded by the work of Holder whose *Elements of Speech* was published in 1669 by the Royal Society. Holder was influenced by the English empiricist tradition and made observations on phonetics and pronunciation, identifying consonant differences and vocalic differences. English grammar took the Latin grammar as its basis, but the empiricist tradition of observation helped them to test and modify this grammar according to the actual patterns and structures of English.

At this time too there was a debate on different approaches to grammar. As Robins (1985; p. 126) writes:

> the empiricists stressed the individual variations of particular languages and the need to adjust categories and classes in the light of observations while the rationalists still looked for what was common to all languages below surface distinctions.

This debate still continues in the interest shown by linguists regarding the search for a 'universal grammar'.

4.5 NINETEENTH-CENTURY LINGUISTICS

There were many significant developments in the nineteenth century which prepared the way for the growth of modern linguistics in the twentieth century. As a result of exposure to other linguistic traditions during the age of colonial expansion, there was a great deal of interest in historical and comparative study of languages. Scholars were keen to explore how languages were related to one another and formed distinct language groups or 'families', e.g. the Indo-European. The discovery of the relationship between Sanskrit and the major languages of Europe (through the work of Sir William Jones) was the greatest impetus to historical studies of the European languages, as Western scholars benefitted from the techniques of analysis adopted by the ancient Sanskrit grammarians and used them to describe European languages in a similar way, e.g. Schlegel's essay 'On the Language and the Learning of the Indians' (1808). These studies were necessarily comparative; as they compared the morphology of Sanskrit and other Indo-European languages. The philologists Rask and Grimm initiated some of these studies in which there was a systematic comparison of word forms, and matching of a sound in one language with a sound in another led to an important formulation (known as

Grimm's Law): 'If there is found between two languages agreement in the forms of indispensable words to such an extent that rules of letter changes can be discovered for passing from one to the other, then there is a basic relationship between these languages'. Rask wrote the first systematic grammars of the Old Norse and Old English, and Grimm initiated studies in Germanic linguistics. One of his important contributions has been in devising technical terms for distinctions between 'strong' and 'weak' forms in inflexions, 'ablaut' (vowel gradation) and 'umlaut' (vowel change because of its environmental conditions).

The nineteenth century linguist, von Humboldt wrote insightfully on many linguistic questions. He studied several languages and developed a theory about the essential creativity of human language which all humans have in common; however, the constitution of the formal structure of each individual language is peculiar to the group or community who speaks it. The inner form of a language is the grammatical and semantic structure of a language which imposes rules on the raw material of speech. Partly, it is common to all humans but partly it is different from all other languages. Humboldt also distinguished between languages as being isolating, agglutinative and inflexional according to the processes of change in the structure of words (see Lyons, 1971).

One of the most significant trends in linguistics towards the end of the nineteenth century was the emergence of the **Neogrammarians**. This school of linguists tried to give a scientific basis to historical linguistics, they were against theorizing and in favour of more data collection from actual languages. Their ideas had considerable influence on the American linguists such as Bloomfield and Sapir. The neogrammarians gave importance to two areas of linguistics: phonetics and dialectology (Robins, 1969; p. 180). Descriptive phonetics based on data from living languages and the process of language change that led to the formation of distinct dialects was studied, and the making of dialect atlases and surveys was initiated. Much of this work took place in Germany, and was the subject of much discussion and controversy.

4.6 LINGUISTICS IN THE TWENTIETH CENTURY

The study of the sound systems of languages by phoneticians and comparative linguists in the nineteenth century prepared the way for a descriptive approach to language, that is, for description of the structure of language. Many languages that had been hitherto undescribed were now being described at the level of their sound systems, and, taking cue from the methods of Sanskrit phoneticians, attempts were made to distinguish the sound system from the alphabet system (as, for example, in the case of English). It was felt that the sound system of any language could be described if linguists had a standard notation for the transcription of speech sounds based on a classification of sounds into vowel and consonant types, each sound being characterised by its place and manner of articulation and given a particular symbol. This set of symbols could then be used to describe the speech sounds of any language. The need for such a notation as a means of transcription of speech sounds led to the devising of the International Phonetic Alphabet (IPA), towards the end of the nineteenth century.

Among the several phoneticians who were concerned with spelling reform, description of speech sounds, acoustics and the devising of phonetic symbols, a prominent one was Henry Sweet. In his *Handbook of Phonetics* (1877), he distinguished between distinctive or contrastive sounds—a distinctive sound being contrasted and set off against another sound is a phoneme (though Sweet did not use this term which came into use later to define a minimal contrasted sound unit). Subsequently, Daniel Jones used this distinction of English words in his *Outline of English Phonetics* (1914).

This work in phonetics was part of an overall shift in emphasis from historical to structural, descriptive linguists, which was synchronic in approach. This shift occurred in Europe spearheaded by the ideas of the Swiss Linguist Ferdinand de Saussure as well as the work of the Prague School in Czechoslovakia. Simultaneously there were studies in American linguistics that followed the structural approach.

4.7 THE AMERICAN STRUCTURALISTS AND BLOOMFIELD

Some of the most important influences on linguistics in the earlier part of the twentieth century came from fields such as anthropology and psychology. Anthropological studies of tribes such as the American Indians (or 'Red Indians' as they were called) revealed the existence of languages with elaborate sound systems which could be studied and described just as Latin and other European languages had been described. This also focussed attention on the structures of word-formation and morphology in different languages. The American anthropologists Boas and Sapir gave a comprehensive description of American-Indian languages such as the languages of the Algonkian family, and thus laid down the basic methodology of modern descriptive linguistics. Their concern was also with the significance of language in human thought and culture and the fundamental link between language and culture.

However, it was felt that only that part of a language can be described which is observable and concrete, i.e. sounds can be observed as they are concrete physiological activities leading to the production of sound-waves but meanings are abstract and cannot be observed. This belief was based on the behaviourist school of psychology, according to which only that mental process which is manifest in behaviour can be scientifically observed and can become the basis of valid scientific conclusions. Since language is also a form of behaviour, its external aspect, i.e. speech, is the focus of linguistic description.

These influences were instrumental in the growth of American structuralism in the first half of the twentieth century. Foremost among the linguists of this school is Leonard Bloomfield. In his seminal book *Language* (1933), he defines and delimits the area of linguistic enquiry. He rejects the universalist ideas about language on the basis that each individual language has its classes and categories; therefore, the only useful generalizations about language are inductive generalizations'.

Applying the behaviourist approach, Bloomfield explains language as a pattern of stimulus and response ($S \rightarrow R$). He posits a situation where there is a stimulus from the external world (*S*) which gives rise to an actual response in the form of an action (*R*). For instance, if a person is hungry and sees an apple, this (the apple) is the stimulus. If he takes the apple and eats it, this is a response. But if, instead of performing an action, he utters some sounds such as 'I am hungry, bring me that apple', this is a speech response (*r*) to the stimulus (*S*) of hunger ($S \rightarrow r$). This in turn may become a speech stimulus (*s*) for the other person, the hearer who may then respond either with an actual action (of getting the apple) as response (*R*) or a speech act (*r*). Therefore, the pattern will be $s \rightarrow R$, or $s \rightarrow r$. Speech stimuli are substitute stimuli and speech responses are substitute responses (i.e. they substitute for the action). Subsequently, Bloomfield focused on the physiological and acoustic characteristics of the speech act, showing that it is verbal behaviour following a pattern of the stimulus and response leading to habit-formation through repetition and imitation.

Bloomfield did not address the larger questions of language and culture as Sapir did, though he took many examples from the linguistic data obtained by the anthropological linguists. As Trager comments, whereas Sapir's concerns were 'macro', Bloomfield's were 'micro', aimed at defining fundamental concepts such as 'phoneme', 'allophone', 'morph', 'morpheme' and 'allomorph'. These definitions were based on the notion of distinctive features. For instance, his definition of morpheme as 'a linguistic form which bears no partial phonetic or semantic resemblance to any other form'. As semantic resemblance is required for distinguishing between morphemes, Bloomfield does not totally exclude meaning. However, the emphasis in his approach lies on the observable and clearly definable aspects of meaning in the same way as at the levels of sounds and syntax.

In a lucid expository style, Bloomfield gives an explanation of morphology and processes of word-formation such as affixation and compounding (distinguishing between analytic and synthetic compounds), drawing examples from English as well as Sanskrit morphology. In an analytic account of sentence structure, Bloomfield gave the concept of 'immediate constituents', according to which a sentence can be broken up into its constituent forms (since the sentence contains them or is constituted of them). Thus, a sentence such as 'Poor John ran away' can be broken up into two immediate constituents 'Poor John' and 'ran away'. Each constituent can subsequently be analysed further, with 'Poor John' consisting of 'Poor' and 'John', and 'ran away' consisting of 'ran' and 'away'. Constituents are grouped on the basis of substitutability, e.g. the whole of the constituent 'Poor John' can be replaced by 'He', similarly the whole constituent 'ran away' can be replaced by 'went'. Thus a constituent is a slot in which similar constituents can be substituted. The notion of dependency or immediacy of the constituents becomes clear when we see that 'Poor' is closer to 'John' than it is to 'ran' and 'away'. The first or immediate connection is between 'Poor' and 'John', and the whole of this constituent 'Poor John' is the immediate constituent of the whole constituent 'ran away'.

Some limitations of Bloomfield's approach are obvious—it is a purely mechanistic explanation and does not take into account the creativity and variability of language. The descriptive approach of Bloomfield, Hockett and others represents the thinking of the American structuralists in the first half of the twentieth century, which was influential till another phase of linguistic studies was initiated by Chomsky in 1957, after which the behaviourist school ceased to be popular and emphasis shifted to devising a theory of language. However, the methods of description and analysis, developed by these structuralists continued to be adopted by linguists to provide systematic and precise accounts of phonology and syntax in various languages.

Of the later American structuralists, Z. Harris attempted to find discovery procedures for a theory of grammar through the process of analysing data, and Pike developed the notion of immediate constituents in a method of grammatical analysis called tagmemics, which is the analysis of grammatical units according to the functions they perform, and brings in the aspect of meaning into syntactic functioning.

4.8 THE CONTRIBUTION OF SAUSSURE

At the same time that structuralist approaches were being taken up in the USA, there were similar developments in Europe. Chief among these was the work of Swiss linguist Ferdinand de Saussure. Saussure's *Course in General Linguistics* (1916) ushered in a revolution in linguistics and in the understanding of the structure of language. He made several important distinctions in the area of language study that set the foundation for the modern structural approach to language—the distinctions between **langue** and **parole**, synchronic and diachronic, form and substance (see Chapter 3). Saussure also introduced the concept of language as a system of signs. This concept became important not only for the understanding of language but also for the understanding of all human and social structures as sign systems.

The sign consists of two elements: the signifier (e.g. a word) and the signified (the concept or meaning). The sign is a composite of both elements in relationship with each other, and is the central fact of language. The relationship between signifier and signified is arbitrary, which means that there is no essential or logical connection between the two. As each language has a different and arbitrary way of organising the world into concepts, each language produces a different set of signifieds. The signifier-signified relationship is established by social agreement, therefore, language is essentially social and has the authority of social convention.

According to Saussure (1916):

> If we could embrace the sum of word-images stored in the minds of all individuals, we could identify the social bond that constitutes language. Language is a storehouse filled by the members of a given community through their active use of speaking, a grammatical system that has a potential existence in each brain, or, more specifically, in the brains of a group of individuals. For language is not complete in any speaker; it exists perfectly only within a collectivity. In separating language from speaking, we are separating what is social from what is individual, what is necessary from what is accidental.

This is the distinction between **langue** (the collective, social, homogenous, stable aspect of language) and **parole** (the individual, variable, heterogeneous aspect of language). Saussure explained that the entire linguistic system can be reduced to a set of syntagmatic and paradigmatic relations and in this sense language is a system of elements wholly defined by their relations to one another within the system (e.g. while /p/, /æ/ and /t/ are in syntagmatic relation, each phoneme is also in paradigmatic relation. /p/ relates to /b/, /æ/ to /ɪ/, /t/ to /d/). The linguistic system consists of different levels of structure and at each level we can identify elements which contrast with one another and combine with other elements to form higher-level units and the principles of structure at each level are fundamentally the same. Language is a system in which elements are identified not by themselves but by their place within the system.

All these explanations made the structural basis of language clear, and gave a definite direction to structural analysis of language as well as literature, folklore etc. Though we now have sociolinguistic evidence that **parole** too is socially restricted, and that **langue** is subject to change, de Saussure's ideas based on this dichotomy have inspired much of the later thinking in linguistics. Saussure's contribution is that he explained the nature of language more clearly and systematically than any linguist before him had done.

4.9 THE PRAGUE SCHOOL

The Prague school consisted of a group of linguists who met regularly in the Czech capital Prague in the twenties and thirties, under the leadership of Count Trubetskoy, a professor from Vienna, and the author of *Principles of Phonology* (1939). These linguists applied Saussure's concepts of phonology. The phoneme concept was elaborated by considering the phoneme as a complex phonological unit which is realised concretely in a speech sound. This unit has distinctive features that characterise it as a separate entity, e.g. the English phonemes /p/ and /b/ being distinguished by the opposition of voiceless/voiced, each sound is distinguished from others because of difference in one or more features. Other contrasts in phonemes occur according to the different positions occupied by them in words, i.e. whether they occur initially, medially or finally. These phonologists also investigated the demarcation of syllable and word boundaries.

Other major theorists of this school include Jakobson who studied Russian phonology and discovered that there are a limited number of phonological features selected by a language. Along with the structural, the Prague school linguists also emphasised the functional aspects of grammar, e.g. Mathesius made statements of all relationship between the grammatical and informational part of the sentence which was characterised as 'theme' and 'rheme' respectively as the 'given' and 'new' information. A combination of the structural and functional approaches also led the Prague linguistics to consider the functions of language in literary texts, and they initiated studies in stylistics.

4.10 LATER DEVELOPMENTS

Of the major developments in linguistics in the post-Bloomfield and post-world war era, the most significant is the development of the transformational-generative approach to language first enunciated by Chomsky in *Syntactic Structures* (1957). This approach overcomes the limitations of Bloomfield's immediate constituent approach which did not explain discontinuity, ambiguity and transformation in sentence structure. Chomsky does this by focusing on a native speaker's knowledge of his own language, which he calls 'competence'. It contains the knowledge of basic structures together with the rules for transforming these structures into a number of transformations. This explains the native speaker's ability to generate an infinite number of actual sentences. The characteristic of this approach is that it integrates semantic, syntactic and phonological levels. Though it incorporates detailed rules for the basic structures and transformations of sentences (known as the phrase structure rules), it is not merely analytic or descriptive, it provides a powerful theory explaining language creativity and transformation.

While in USA Chomsky led this revolution in grammar, in UK, linguists like J.R. Firth, a Professor of Linguistics in London, also addressed language description in relation to meaning and context. He gave the idea of 'context of situation' which is that utterances (composed of words and phrases) are functional in particular situational contexts. Firth also contributed to phonology in giving an account of prosodic phonology, i.e. connected speech in which the articulation of syllables and words is affected by factors such as stress, juncture and intonation (also known as supra segmental features). Firth's ideas were developed by the neo-Firthian school led by Halliday and others who worked out the details of the functional grammar suggested by Firth into an elaborate account of syntax known as **scale and category grammar**. This grammar links grammatical (formal) features to function in context.

In recent years there has also been a tremendous development in the areas of semantics, sociolinguistics and the analysis of discourse. Earlier, the Saussurian distinction between **langue** and **parole** excluded the study of the latter, but in the work of linguists such as Fishman, Hymes (who gave the definition of communicative competence) and Labov, this distinction becomes blurred, as **parole** also shows elements of systematicity and regularity occurring even in language variation. Linguists have been analysing the social and conventional rules underlying conversation and discourse—both spoken and written—to achieve a better understanding of language use in communication. Though many aspects of language are now understood, the voyage of discovery continues, building on the centuries of study done by linguists on the complex phenomena of human language. This is part of the enterprise of knowledge, i.e. 'know thyself', for knowing about language means knowing about ourselves.

SUMMARY

The foundations of linguistics can be traced to ancient times. Of the older linguistic traditions, the most significant are:

The Indian tradition. The chief contribution to this was made by grammarians and phonologists of Sanskrit, such as Panini and Patanjali, as well as scholars of poetics such as Bharathari. They discussed concepts such as 'dhvani' and 'sphota' and 'sandhi' in phonology and morphology.

The Greek and Roman traditions. Spanning several centuries, these traditions began with philosophers like Plato and Aristotle, and continued with grammarians such as Thrax, Priscian and Donatus. Their contributions were mainly in the study of grammar on the basis of classical texts of Greek and Latin, e.g. the definition of word classes, sentence types, morphological description.

In the modern age after the Renaissance, European languages such as French and German were studied extensively. Interest grew in the comparative study of languages and the establishment of language families. Though in the initial stages the emphasis of study was on the writing of grammars and dictionaries, phonology developed towards the end of the nineteenth century.

Linguistics in the twentieth century was influenced by anthropology and the behaviourist school of psychology. While on one hand, many languages other than the European were brought under scrutiny, on the other hand methods of description of language became more rigorous and data-based. The development of the International Phonetic Alphabet, of concepts of 'phoneme' and 'morpheme' and of constituent structure of sentences gave new thrusts to the areas of phonology and grammar. In the later half of the century, the theory of transformational-generative grammar provided a new paradigm for study of language. Important linguists in this century, to name only a few, are Bloomfield, Harris, de Saussure, Count Trubetskoy, Roman Jakobson, Noam Chomsky, J.R. Firth and Michael Halliday.

COMPREHENSION QUESTIONS

1. What are the main contributions made by the Sanskrit grammarians of ancient India?
2. 'The main difference between ancient and modern linguistics is that while the former took as its basis the texts by classical writers, the latter takes actual language data as its basis'. Discuss how approaches to language have changed during the history of linguistics in the light of this statement.
3. From your reading of this chapter, can you reach some conclusions regarding the manner in which the science of linguistics has grown? Does it follow a linear pattern and is there evidence of how various schools and approaches have influenced each other?
4. What advances in modern linguistics have brought about major changes in our awareness of language?

CHAPTER 5

The Study of Language Variation

5.1 INTRODUCTION

Everybody knows that the English we read in the newspapers today or hear on the radio or the television is not the same today as it was several hundred years ago. It is quite possible that a modern reader of English may not be able to understand a single line from a paper written one thousand years ago. For example, here is a partial specimen selected from the Lord's Prayer ("Our Father") written in Old English, more than one thousand years ago:

"f æ dər urə ...

... forgyf us ure gyltas".

Changes in language are bound to occur as change is natural. Language is a manifestation of human behaviour; it cannot be static and fixed, the same for all times. Change is, no doubt, a very slow but sure process. It sometimes goes unnoticed and becomes markedly prominent only over a long period of time.

Some of the language changes can be linked to major political and social events (e.g., wars, invasions, other upheavals) bringing about major changes in the living style of communities using the language. Apart from this, one must not forget that change in language is a natural process also. Language seems to be in a state of continual transition because of its cultural transmission from one generation to the next. Each new generation has to find a way of using or learning the language of the previous generation.

In this continuous process, each new language user has to 'recreate' for himself or herself the language of the community. He is able to pick up some elements exactly, but he picks up other elements only approximately and thus brings about a change. Also, there is an occasional desire to 'sound' different from the previous generation. You can mark the change in the way the words undergo changes in their meaning and use from the changes the word for "a place meant to defecate or urinate" has undergone: latrine, toilet, WC, wash room, rest room, relaxing room, or just 'gents'/'ladies' and so on. Thus we find that change is something invisible in language. This change is natural, neither for good nor for bad, but as per the suitability, needs and whims of the users of a language.

Language change or variations in language can be studied along two dimensions: *Diachronic* (or historical) and *Synchronic* (at a particular period of time).

English used by Chaucer differs radically from the variety used by Milton, and both these differ from that found in T.S. Eliot. There is a marked difference between old English (Anglo-Saxon), Middle English and Modern English. Indeed the difference is huge. These three varieties illustrate language variations that have been taking place in English during the course of history. These language variations are diachronic variations. As students of descriptive linguistics what is more important to us is language variations along the synchronic dimension. Variations in language at a given period of time are synchronic variations. There is no doubt that there are innumerable varieties of English.

We shall first study some diachronic changes that have taken place in English language and then take up the synchronic variations.

5.2 SOME DIACHRONIC VARIATIONS IN LANGUAGE

Here is a select list of examples of variations in English that have taken place in course of time in its progress from Old English to Middle English, and then to Modern English.

1. The meaning of a word may be *changed* as a result of its repeated use in a particular kind of context. Sometimes a change results from a word retaining its original form, but its meaning changes because the object it stood for has changed, e.g., originally 'pen' stood for *feather*. Later *feathers* were used for writing (quill pen). So, *pen* acquired a new meaning.
2. **Extension** has taken place in a large number of English words, e.g., *journey* originally meant a "day's walk/ride", and a *journal* was a periodical that appeared "every day". Now a journey may be a week's journey or a half yearly journal.
3. Transition of proper name to common words may also result in changes, e.g., the word '*boycott*' is derived from Captain Charles C. Boycott (1832–97) who was a land agent of Lord Erne's estate, who was so treated in an attempt to get rents reduced. The word '*dunce*' owes its origin to the name of a medieval writer, Duns Scotus who fell into disrepute.
4. **Euphemism**: One seeks to disguise the real nature of an unpleasant idea by giving it an inoffensive name, e.g., *bathroom* or *restroom* for "toilet" (or latrine), stout for "fat", visually challenged for blind, etc.
5. In Modern English, the front vowels are not rounded whereas most of the back vowels are rounded, but in Early English, there were front *rounded* vowels:

Old English	**Middle English**	**Modern English**
[r ą d]	[rɔ:d]	[rəʊd]
[h ą m]	[hɔ:m]	[həʊm]

6. **Metathesis** could be seen in operation in some words:

Old English	**Middle English**
brid	bird

7. Loss of /r/ medially before consonants and finally (unless the next word begins with a vowel) took place in the 18th century although r was retained in spellings, e.g., arm, heard, order.
8. Initial /k/ and /g/ followed by n, disappeared in *pronunciation* in the late 17th century, e.g., *knave, gnaw, gnat, gnash.*
9. **Spelling**: A major reason for the variety of English spelling is that several different systems/conventions have been at work in this language, e.g., 'Mouse' is the native spelling. 'Mice' is a French spelling, made possible by the fact that old French (s) became (c) next to front vowels.
10. There were no silent letters in OE.

Old English	**Modern English**
Cnight	Knight (K silent)

11. Under French influence, many old English spellings were changed, e.g.,
    (a) e o remained in spellings but became a monophthong, e.g., people.
    (b) y was often used to represent '(i)' e.g., myhte (might), wys (wise).
    (c) Modern English brought reforms in spelling, e.g., dropping of the final *e* in many words.
12. **Accidence**: The history of English accidence has been one of progressive simplification, e.g, several declensions of nouns in OE have disappeared today. Inflexional endings of adjectives/adverbs were also simplified in the course of time.
13. **Syntax**: Old English prose is undisciplined. Change of construction in the middle of sentence is quite common. Some sentences begin in the third person, but continue in the first person.

Modern syntax is *more logical.* This can be seen in our attitude to double comparatives, double negatives and double superlatives. Modern English gives more importance to *word order.* Confusion between the use of *shall* and *will* has given way to 'll.

5.3 SYNCHRONIC VARIATIONS

Synchronic variations of English can be studied under three headings:

- Varieties due to language contact
- Varieties of dialect
- Varieties of register

5.31 Varieties due to Language Contact

It often happens that a language comes in contact with another language. This gives rise to new varieties of language that continue to co-exist along with the original languages. In modern sociolinguistics, these are also known as 'transplanted', nativized' or 'indigenized' varieties. Some of the varieties of English are:

(i) Indian English

Indian English is a general term that applies to any variety of English, spoken in any region of India, e.g., Tamilian English, Maharashtrain English, Bengali English, and so on. There is no uniformly consistent standard Indian English spoken all over the country. That is why good or educated speakers in English in India try to approximate, as far as possible, to received pronunciation (RP) of UK. It is in this process that a variety of regional English have come up, all vaguely termed *Indian English*. An attempt was made at Central Institute of English and Foreign Languages (CIEFL), Hyderabad by Dr R.K. Bansal to evolve an Indian variety of English known as GIE–General Indian English. In the GIE, for example, he introduced sounds like:

RP	GIE
/θ/	[t̪h]
/eɪ/	[e:]
/əʊ/	[o:]
/ð/	[d̪]

Apart from phonology, there are lexical and grammatical items that characterize this variety of English. Some examples are:

LEXICAL	INDIAN ENGLISH	BRITISH ENGLISH
	bed tea	morning tea
	hill station	hill resort
	bus stop	bus station
	cousin brother/sister	cousin
	biodata	curriculum vitae

Indian English includes *hybrid compounds*, such as those made out of a combination of English and Hindi, e.g., policewallah, brahminhood, etc.

Syntactic

Word order of questions remains unchanged, e.g. "Where you are going"? instead of "Where are you going"? In Hindi, questions are marked by change in intonation, not by syntactic change.

Invariant question tags, e.g. 'You are going tomorrow, isn't it?' instead of 'aren't you?'

These are some features that show that Indian English is well on the way to becoming a variety of English with a distinct structure at all levels. However, no standard dictionary has so far been written for any General Indian English. This is why even some educated speakers of English in India think that the term *Indian English* stands for a mixed language made up of several regional varieties (in respect of sound, syntax or usage) of English.

(ii) Pidgin language

'Pidgin language' is a special language with a very limited vocabulary and limited structures, used for purposes like trade, etc. by those people who have no common language between themselves. Such pidgin languages have come up to be used at several places where speakers of two different languages meet for specific purposes, e.g., fish traders of India and Sri Lanka; in habitants of West Indies and Pacific islands.

Such pidgin languages were also called 'bazaar' languages. In the islands of West Indies and the Pacific, pidgins continue to be the languages spoken even when the initial purpose of trade no more existed. Some examples of pidgin are: 'I go go market' (Cameroon pidgin). 'I chowchow' for 'I eat' (Chinese pidgin), 'plenty man' for 'many men' (Melanesian pidgin).

(iii) Creole

When a pidgin language comes to be used for a long period by a community as a whole and it develops its own vocabulary and structures, it becomes a *Creole*. It is the product of two different languages originally used by the speakers.

A Creole may arise when a pidgin becomes the first language of the community, and begins to be used in a wider range of communicative functions. It becomes a new, restructured system, though it may still not be used in very formal contexts. Examples are: Jamaican creole, Haitian creole, etc. New words appear in creoles, e.g., 'zozo' for 'bird', 'fingafoot' for 'toe', 'pikin' for 'child' and so on.

(iv) Esperanto

Esperanto is a theoretical language to be used by all people all over the world. Some people continue to make an attempt to evolve such a world language, based on the vocabulary and codes of important languages in the world. However, so far, no such attempts has been successful.

5.32 Varieties of Dialect

The variety of a language according to the user is called *Dialect*. It is determined by a *speaker's* (user's) *social and geographical background*. Language may vary on the geographical plane from one region to another. This is why it is difficult to talk about a single entity called British English. In Britain, there are numerous dialects of English according to the area where these are spoken, e.g. the Lancashire dialect, the Scottish dialect, the Yorkshire dialect, and so on. The same is true of American English too.

Dialectical variations are also determined by *social hierarchy* and *social class*. The aristocrat in London, for example, uses one variety of English and the lower class uses another variety. The so-called RP (Received Pronunciation) used to be the dialect of the upper class society of England, although it has now expanded its regional and social boundaries. Dialects are at times conditioned by *religion and caste* also. Also, within the same religion, 'dialectal' differences are conditioned by caste, for example, the Namboodri (the highest Hindu, Brahmin of Kerala) dialect.

This means that within a given language we have a number of dialects. Between two dialects there may be grammatical, lexical and phonological differences, even though they may have the same core system of language in common, e.g. General American English and RP are two different dialects of English. They differ in many ways, as the examples below show:

1. Phonological level differences

	RP	**General American**
Last	/la : st/	/læst/
Dance	/da: ns/	/dæns/
Missile	/'mɪsdɪl/	/'mɪsɪl/
Class	/kla:s/	/klæs/
Vitamin	/vɪtəmɪn/	/vaɪtəmɪn/

2. Differences at the level of syntax

US	**British**
different than	different from
check that out	check up on that
to talk with somebody	to talk to somebody

3. Lexical differences

Gas	Petrol
Candy	Chocolate
Elevator	Lift
Jelly	Jam

4. Morphology

dive-dove	dive-dived
(past)	(past)

5. Graphology (spelling)

Program	Programme
color	colour
realize	realise

Dialect map

On the basis of such differences in phonology, morphology, syntax, etc., it is possible to draw imaginary boundaries separating the geographical areas using divergent linguistic items. The boundary line that separates the users of one area using a particular linguistic item from the area using the other linguistic item is called an *Isogloss*.

We can draw a number of isoglosses in a similar fashion. All such isoglosses may not coincide. A large number of such isoglosses may overlap and from a sort of *bundle*. The phenomenon is called *bundling*. A bundle of isoglosses is considered a *dialect boundary* (see Fig. 5.1). Maps of this sort (e.g. one shown above) are called *dialect maps*.

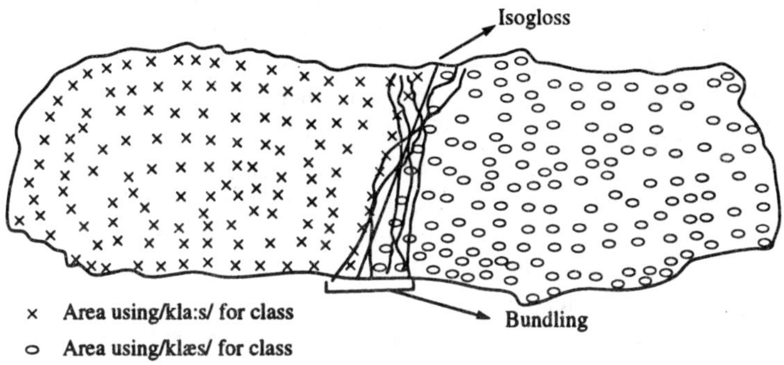

Fig. 5.1 Dialect boundary.

Dialect dictionary

Since dialects are now being studied in greater detail (dialectology), the lexicons of these dialects have been compiled. Such a lexicon is called a *dialect dictionary*.

Sociolect: A social dialect or a class dialect used by the members of a particular group of a speech community is called *Sociolect*. For example, *slang*, used by young people.

Diglossia: Sometimes a speech community uses two dialects, but there is a strong tendency to use one of these for special, prestigious or formal occasions. This prestigious dialect is called *high*, and the informal, commonly spoken dialect is called *low*. These two are not allowed to intermingle. Such a use of two dialects by a speech community is called *Diglossia*, e.g., 'high' and 'low' Tamil, 'high' and 'low' Arabic.

Idiolect: Within a given dialect one may find differences of speech between individuals. No two speaker speak exactly alike. The term 'idiolect' is used to refer to the idiosyncracies of an individual speaker.

These peculiarities can be those of pronunciation, grammar, vocabulary, etc. "Idiolect is the individual's personal variety of the community language system" (Crystal). Language variations are present in individuals as much as in societies, and they can become regular and systematic in terms of the individual's own use of the linguistic code. Though the notion of idiolect and style may overlap, idiolect is different from style in the sense that style is more often a matter of choice. A person's style can vary in different situations of speech and writing, e.g. a poet may choose one type of style for one poem and another style for other poems. Idiolect is consistent over the whole of an individual's use of the language and is often like an unconscious mannerism. For example, Uriah Heep's repeated use of he word 'umble' in Dicken's *David Copperfield* is an instance of that character's idiolect: the character is identified by the use of that item of speech.

Language and dialect

It is sometimes very difficult to say whether A and B are different languages or just different dialects of the same language. The partial solution to this problem is provided by the concept of mutual intelligibility. If two speakers are mutually intelligible, they are using the same language even if they are using different dialects. If they are not intelligible to each other, they are using different languages. It is, in fact, difficult to draw rigid boundary lines between languages. At times dialects of the same language may be so divergent that speakers of the same language may find each other mutually unintelligible.

A dialect rises to the status of a language when a community speaking a certain dialect is politically and socially powerful. The speakers may manage to force the government to acknowledge their variety as a separate language (that is why it is often said that a language is a dialect with an army and a navy). The Hindi dialect popular in Western UP became the national language of the country (India) because an influential group of leaders in free India belonged to that area.

5.33 Register

The same individual uses different varieties of a language depending upon the *situation*. This language according to the situation is called *register*.

The kind of language that a lecturer uses in a classroom is not the kind of English that he uses in the kitchen, talking to his wife or the kind of English he uses on the stage in a Convocation function. One uses different registers in talking to one's wife, one's colleague, and one's boss. Consider Mr. John speaking to his wife, then to a colleague, and then to his boss:-

To wife: Met that fool Jolly today. Wants his job back, can you imagine?

To colleague: Do you remember Jolly Smith? I met him today and he said he'd like his job back. I think he is too optimistic, do you?

To boss: I met Mr. Jolly Smith yesterday, sir, who used to work in the stores. He asked me to find out if he could again join his post. I only said I'II pass on your request and find out the position. Should he have any hopes, sir?

These are three different *registers* used by Mr. John. He uses an informal register while talking to his wife, but a formal register while talking to his boss. We talk of formal register, the informal register, the register of linguistics, the register of law, the literary register, the register of commerce, science, and so on.

5.34 Classification of Registers

(i) *Register according to the field of discourse* (or the purpose and the subject matter of communication)

Such registers include the register of science, the register of law, register of religion, the register of journalism, etc. Some examples are listed.

The register of science: Equal volumes of all gases, under similar conditions of temperature and pressure, contain equal number of molecules.

The register of journalism: Girish, 46, and his wife 39, residents of Lovers' Lane, Ludhiana, escaped with minor injuries when a powerful bomb planted in their garage exploded seconds after the couple locked the garage soon after sunset yesterday.

The register of religion: O Lord our heavenly Father! We pray to Thee to have mercy on thy people.

(ii) *Register according to the mode of discourse*

These refer to the register variations determined by the medium (spoken or written) used. We can talk about different varieties of language in a telegraphic message, telephone conversation, a mobile message, a radio, television or newspaper. We can also have differences between the spoken language and the written language.

EXAMPLES: (i) Arriving tomorrow, prepare reception (a telegraphic message)

(ii) Hello! It is Ramesh, O, Bhabhi – what a pleasant surprise ! When did you arrive? Where is the Boss ? O.K. I'll be there. (A telephonic conversation)

(iii) *Register according to the style or tenor of discourse*: These refer to the relation [*to whom*] between the speaker and the addressee. These registers include the formal style, the informal style, the frozen style, the colloquial style, the intimate style, etc.

EXAMPLES: (Taken from Strevens)

Frozen style: Those seeking an interview should make their way at once to the upper floor by way of the staircase.

Formal style: Interview seekers should go up the stairs at once.

Casual: Time you all went upstairs, now.

Intimate: Up you go, chaps.

Notice that the field of discourse, the mode of discourse, and the style of discourse are not mutually exclusive. A lecture on Biology in a science class, for example, will be in a scientific *field*, lecturing *mode* and a formal polite *style*.

5.35 Some Distinctions

(i) *Register and dialect*

Register	*Dialect*
1. These are variations of use.	1. These are variations according to the user.
2. A single speaker may use a number of registers for different situations.	2. A single speaker is normally in command of a single dialect.

Register	Dialect
3. Register is determined by the situation in which a speaker is.	3. A dialect is determined by the speaker's background.
4. Register is conditioned by the situations and need of a speaker.	4. Dialect is determined by caste, region, social status, etc.
5. Register shows what your are doing.	5. Dialect shows who (or what) you are.

(ii) *Dialect and accent*

Dialect	*Accent*
Dialect is a combination of all levels of the language, the use of which serves to identify the speaker's regional social group. It includes pronunciation, grammar and vocabulary.	Accent is limited to one area of the language, i.e. pronunciation, which identifies the speaker's regional or social group, e.g. British RP (Received Pronunciation).

Note that the notion of accent overlaps with that of dialect. Variation occurring at all levels defines a dialect. Within it, features of accent, i.e. phonological features may sometimes be given more importance as a mark of a speaker's regional or class background (often the two are linked). For instance, class distinctions in Britain ensured that the RP accent became associated with a particular class and any variation from RP began to signal a difference in social status and hence was looked down upon.

(iii) *Dialect and language*

Dialect	*Language*
1. A dialect is smaller, confined in its range to a smaller area.	1. A language is larger in range and size.
2. A dialect is used for limited number of functions and rarely in official, administrative and educational contexts.	2. A language is used for a greater number of functions in different contexts.
3. A dialect often does not have official status.	3. It has official status.
4. A dialect is not codified in formal writing, in grammars and dictionaries and may not have a written literature.	4. It is codified and standardized, in writing, grammars and dictionaries, and has a written literature.
5. It is often considered less prestigious	5. It has social prestige.

5.4 STYLISTIC STUDY OF LITERATURE

Stylistics is that branch of linguistics which takes the language of literary texts as its object of study. Out of the many types of variation that occur in language, it is the variation in literary style that is most complex, and thus offers unlimited scope for linguistic analysis. The study of style is important in literature as each literary text is an individual use of language reflecting the unique personality and thoughts of the writer. In literary criticism, it is said that "style is the man". Every writer uses language in his or her own way, making changes and variations at each level of the language: word choice, sentence structure and sound patterns.

Stylistics is different from literary criticism in the following way: It is a systematic study of features of style and variations in style at each level of language structure. It is true that stylistics does have something in common with traditional rhetoric. For example, the study of features such as rhyme scheme, metre, diction, figures of speech such as metaphor, simile, etc., was done by literary scholars even in ancient times. Particular attention was given to these devices in poetry, as these were considered as part of the aesthetic appreciation of poetry. Since all these devices involve some manipulation of language, they are also important for linguists. However, just an observation of some rhetorical features is not enough for the modern stylistician. First and foremost, the stylistic study of literature involves the following:

1. A detailed description of each linguistic feature at each level. The phonological level includes the combinations of individual sounds and the patterns of syllables that make up the metre. The level of syntax includes the ordering of items in the sentence, and the length and complexity of clauses and phrases. Diction studies the choice of particular words and of synonyms, antonyms, etc. At the semantic level, the extension and association of meaning through the use of ambiguity, substitution, etc., form the focus of attention.
2. A description of those features which are prominent in the text, because (a) they are repeated, (b) they are placed at prominent positions, or (c) they depart from the given grammatical rules of the language.
3. Analysis of all these components enables the stylistician to reach some conclusion regarding the particular nature and qualities of the literary work and pinpoints the variations that make it different from other works.

Stylistics in modern times came up through the work of linguists like Roman Jacobson, who applied the ideas of Saussure to the language of literature. Jacobson refers to the paradigmatic and syntagmatic relationships in language as explained by Saussure and shows that, in literary use of language, those items that are related at the paradigmatic level are shifted to the syntagmatic level. Literary language upsets the normal syntagmatic sequence in some way and thus becomes different from ordinary language. This is so even when there is some extra pattern or regularity in the sentence, e.g. "The cat sat on the mat" has three items which are related on a level of paradigmatic similarity at the phonological level (i.e. similar sounds). These items are placed in a sequence so that the parallelism of sound becomes a prominent feature of this sentence. This is a simple example of how poetic rhythm is created. Other examples of alliteration, rhyme, and so on also work on the same principle of equivalence at the phonological level. The same holds for other levels, e.g. the repetition of words and sentences also creates **parallelism**.

Another such shift from ordinary language is seen when the grammatical rules are not followed and some item which does not normally occupy a particular position in a sentence is made to do so. For example, 'pretty how town' has one adjective that is normal in relation to the noun, but the second item 'how' is not normally used in adjective position. This is called a **deviation.** Literary style is full of such deviations. For instance, metaphor is also an example of a deviation since a meaning is given to an item which is not normally its meaning, e.g. "The *ship ploughed* the deep".

Both parallelism and deviation occur at several levels in a literary text, simultaneously at the levels of phonology, syntax and semantics. Let us take the following lines:

> Home is the hunter, home from the hill
> And the sailor home from the sea.

Here, parallelism exists at the phonological level in the repetition of the sounds 'h' and 's', and at the semantic level in the two parallel sets: hunter = hill, sailor = sea. The repetition of 'home' creates semantic unity and emphasis on the significance of 'home' in contrast to 'hill' and 'sea', which can then be seen as places different and far from 'home'. At the same time, there is deviation in the sentence structure, as the word order is changed in the phrase "home is the hunter", with the subject placed in the end rather than the beginning. So we can see that even in two simple lines of poetry, parallelism and deviation are present.

Both these devices function to create the effect of **foregrounding**. This is a term used by the linguists of the school of Russian Formalism. According to them, foregrounding is the effect of unique features in the text that are different in some way from the normal, and thus stand in contrast to the ordinary language. They become the foreground while the normal language is the background. The style of a literary text is a totality of all such foregrounded elements.

5.41 The Uses of Stylistic Study of Literature

One of the uses of the study of literature is in the interpretation and appreciation of literary texts. Often, judgements about literature have been made impressionistically or subjectively, without providing the evidence for such judgements in the text. Stylistic study provides clear evidence in the text, on the basis of which judgements can be made. The evaluation of the 'greatness' or otherwise of literary works can thus be made on the basis of objective facts of language found in the text itself.

Another use of stylistic study is to establish authorship in cases where it may be doubtful. Comparison of the styles of different authors, or of different texts by the same author, can reveal the particular characteristics of a genre or a period in literary history, e.g. comparison of similar features in some poems can show that they all belong to a certain sub-class of poetry written in a specific age, say, eighteenth century.

Overall, the stylistic study of literature is of interest to the linguist as it reveals variation in language that takes place within certain contextual parameters. It reveals much about the creative and open-ended aspects of language use. Many coinages and expressions used by poets and writers pass into the conventions of the language and may themselves become the norm. Thus, deviation, patterning, etc., are not to be found only in literary texts but also in other areas of language use, e.g. advertising, journalism, political language, and popular songs. This opens up a wide area of language variation and language use which is an interesting object of study for understanding more about language and its role in society.

5.5 THE VALUE OF STUDY OF LANGUAGE VARIATION

In linguistics, we are concerned with the nature of language. In the field of sociolinguistics, it is recognized that there is a relation between language use and social context and social situations. Particular changes come about in the language when it is used in particular social situations, depending on a variety of factors such as the role of the participants, their social status, age, class, gender, and the place of origin. This is how varieties of language are formed, and thus there is a difference between spoken and written English, British and American English, R.P. and dialects of English, formal and informal English, the English used by the young generation and the older generation, and so on.

Sociolinguistics makes us aware that language is not homogeneous. This awareness is most important in the teaching and learning of languages and thus has a considerable role to play in education. The knowledge provided by sociolinguistics is significant in the field of language pedagogy in several ways. Pit Corder writes:

> In preparing a teaching programme we have to take into account what the speakers' needs may be, in terms of the social situations he is going to have to participate in and the social groups he/she may aspire to be part of. This will enable us to set about specifying the linguistic "repertoire" which he/she will need to command. It is this proposed repertoire which forms the basis of a syllabus for the learner.

The significance of study of language variation lies in understanding the purpose for which the learner needs to learn the language. Language is so vast and varied that every learner may not be able to learn everything about it, nor perhaps does he/she need to. For example, a scientist or engineer may need language to work in that particular field, and may not need to learn to use the literary register. Nor would it be economical in terms of the time and resources available to teach such learners those registers that they don't need. Thus, a syllabus can be designed for those learners keeping their needs in view, and this syllabus would contain the vocabulary and structures that are needed. How would the syllabus designer do this? It would not be possible without a thorough knowledge of that particular register. If a course has to be designed for business communication, the syllabus framer must know the features of the variety of language which is used in business communication. This knowledge is essential for all those teachers who design special, need-based courses for learners in different fields. Thus, along with the teaching of some core structures and vocabulary, the learner may have to be taught a range of items from those areas of activity in which he/she is likely to use the language.

The knowledge of language variation is also significant for determining the choice of the model of language to be taught. Since it is acknowledged that any language is not one single whole and that there are many co-existent varieties of a language, the question as to which variety can serve as the model for purposes of teaching is a problematic one.

For the teacher, the knowledge of language varieties is essential since the learners speak different varieties in the classroom. In the days when the method of teaching a language was largely grammar-translation and learners were exposed chiefly to written language, perhaps it was not necessary to acknowledge the varieties that exist. But with the adoption of communicative approaches to language teaching, the learners were required to speak and interact more frequently in the classroom, and they would do so mostly in the variety, e.g. dialect, sub-dialect, class dialect, and idiolect, that they were most familiar with. In earlier times, this may have been frowned upon, but judging a learner's speech during communicative activity is contrary to the principles of the new methodology. The attitude taken by the teacher to differences in language use will have to be more open and tolerant. Since learners come from different social, economic and regional backgrounds, they may be prone to producing errors which are due to the influence of their particular dialect. The teacher who knows this will be able to understand the difficulties of the learners in particular areas, say, some aspects of grammar or pronunciation, and give more attention to such items so that the learner moves ahead in learning the language. At the same time, the learner would recognize that there is nothing bad or wrong about a certain dialectal variety, but that it is appropriate only in certain contexts and not in others. For example, the sentence "I ain't done nothin" may be acceptable (especially as a spoken idiom), and widely used in some contexts and not in others. Pit Corder emphasizes the importance of the learner's acquiring a 'repertory' of alternative forms depending on the situation. The use of the appropriate form constitutes what Dell Hymes (1972) calls "communicative competence". Competence in the structures of the language is not enough for communication; what is also required is competence in use.

It is in this light that grammars such as the Communicative Grammar of English can prove to be useful for teachers and learners. It is both pedagogically and democratically sound to adopt a tolerant attitude in the classroom since it will decrease the learner's anxiety and help learning.

SUMMARY

Everybody knows that the English we come across in the newspapers today or hear on the radio or the television is not the same today as it was several hundred years ago. It is quite possible that a modern reader of English may not be able to understand a single line from a paper written thousand years ago.

Changes in language are bound to occur as change is natural. Language is a manifestation of human behaviour; it cannot be static and fixed, the same for all times. Changes is, no doubt, a very slow but sure process. It sometimes goes unnoticed and becomes markedly prominent only over a long period of time.

Language change or variations in language can be studied along two dimensions: Diachronic (or historical) and Synchronic (at a particular period of time).

English used by Chaucer differs radically from the variety used by Milton, and both these differ from that found in T.S. Eliot. Old English (Anglo-Saxon), Middle English and Modern English differ from one another in a big way. These three varieties illustrate language variations that have been taking place in English during the course of history. These language variations are **diachronic variations**. As students of descriptive linguistics, what is more important to us is language variations along the **synchronic dimension**. Variations in language at a given period of time are synchronic variations. There is no doubt that there are innumerable varieties of English.

Synchronic variations of English can be studied under three heading:

1. Varieties due to language contact
2. Varieties of dialect
3. Varieties of register

It often happens that a language comes in contact with another language. This gives rise to new varieties of language that continue to co-exist along with the original languages. In modern sociolinguistics, these are also known as 'transplanted', 'nativised' or 'indigenised' varieties.

The variety of a language according to the *user* is called 'Dialect'. Dialect is determined by a *speaker's* (user's) *social and geographical background*. Language may vary on the geographical plane from one region to another. This is why it is difficult to talk about a single entity called British English. In Britain, there are numerous dialects of English according to the area where these are spoken, e.g. the Lancashire dialect, the Scotfish dialect, the Yorkshire dialect, and so on. The same is true of American English too.

The same individual uses different varieties of a language depending upon the *situation*. This language according to the situation is called *register*.

The kind of language that a lecturer uses in a classroom is not the kind of English that he uses in the kitchen, talking to his wife or the kind of English he uses on the stage in a Convocation function.

Registers can be classified as follows:

(i) *Register according to the field of discourse* (or the purpose and the subject matter of communication).
Such registers include the register of science, the register of law, register of religion, the register of journalism, etc.

(ii) *Register according to the mode of discourse*: These refer to the register variations determined by the medium (spoken or written) used. We can talk about different varieties of language in a telegraphic message, telephone conversion, a mobile message, a radio, television or newspaper. We can also have differences between the spoken language and the written language.

(iii) *Register according to the style or tenor of discourse*: These refer to the relation [*to whom*] between the speaker and the addressee. These registers include the formal style, the informal style, the frozen style, the colloquial style, the intimate style, and so on.

Note that the field of discourse, the mode of discourse, and the style of discourse are not mutually exclusive. A lecture on Biology in a science class, for example, will be in a scientific *field*, lecturing *mode* and a formal polite *style*.

Idiolect is individual variation, and *style* is variation made according to some conscious purpose, to create particular effects, e.g. the use of sound parallelism to create rhythm. Stylistic variation in language is important in literature. It accounts for the unique aesthetic qualities of a literary work.

The study of language variation is relevant for the teaching and learning of languages, and for developing the learner's communicative ability.

COMPREHENSION QUESTIONS

1. What do you understand by the term 'language variation'. Why do languages change?
2. Distinguish between Diachronic variations and Synchronic variations. Give examples.
3. Write a note on Diachronic variations in language. Give examples from English.
4. What are the different Synchronic variations in language? Explain.
5. Write an essay on: Register, Dialect and Style.
6. Distinguish between:
   - Register and Dialect
   - Regional and Class Dialect
   - Dialect and Language
   - Style and Register
   - Dialect and Accent
   - Idiolect and Style
7. Explain the following:
   - Pidgin language
   - Creole
   - Esperanto
   - Isogloss
   - Bundling
   - Dialect map
   - Idiolect
   - Sociolect
   - Diglossia
   - Deviation
   - Foregrounding
8. List some varieties of language found in your own region, e.g. some dialects of Hindi, the idiom or slang used by the youth, language of newspapers/advertising.

SECTION II

The Study of Grammar

CHAPTER 6

What is Grammar?

6.1 THE BACKGROUND

We may say at the outset itself that it is very difficult to precisely define the term **grammar**. It is difficult to say which came earlier—language or grammar, but common sense leads one to conclude that those who tried to study language must have arrived at some sort of grammar of language. May be, grammar was an attempt to discover certain patterns in language structure, an attempt to classify words and sentences, and then to deduce some 'rules'. It must have been, initially, an attempt to describe language, but those who tried to discover 'rules' or 'patterns' or to classify words or structures assumed a sort of prescriptive authority and came out with normative statements. Modern linguists affirm that any scientific study of language has to be descriptive, not prescriptive.

The question as to what grammar is, continues to remain unanswered. Look at a simple sentence like: "Chess is a game of glorious tricks." The moment somebody says: "Game glorious tricks of is a chess", we happen to remark that it is an ungrammatical or nonsensical sentence. This means, grammaticality has something to do with sense (or meaningfulness) of sentences. It is grammar, therefore, that gives the user of a language the ability to distinguish between a sentence and a non-sentence. Similarly, it is grammar again that makes us see the synonymity or relationship based on identical meaning between sentences like:

Kapil hit a lovely six
and
A lovely six was hit by Kapil.

Every language has its grammar. There is a system in which words join to form meaningful sentences. This does not necessarily mean that 'grammar' is some sort of book containing a detailed statement of any rules. It only means that anybody who speaks or writes acceptable sentences in a language knows its grammar.

Grammar is said to operate between phonology and semantics. Phonology, as is well-known, is the study of the sounds of a language while semantics is the study of meaning. Grammar studies the way in which words/morphemes join to form meaningful sentences. This brings us to the study of syntax which is the basic ingredient of grammar. Grammar tells us the difference between sets of sentences like:

(a) John is easy to please.
John is eager to please.

(b) Ram killed Ravana.
Ravana killed Ram.

Grammar also includes morphology, a study of formation of words. It studies, for example, how words change their forms to express different meanings. An English verb **'take'** for example, takes five different forms: **take, takes, took, taken, taking** to express five different meanings. In Sanskrit, a verb takes nine different forms corresponding to three different persons and tenses in this language. Similar is the case with Latin. All this study of formation of words, different 'inflections' of words, forms a part of any grammatical study.

A study of grammar includes the study of five fundamental units of grammatical structure. These fundamental units are:

1. Morpheme
2. Word
3. Phrase
4. Clause
5. Sentence

It would be worthwhile to explain these terms in brief:

Morpheme is the lowest unit amongst the five fundamental units of grammatical description if they are placed in rank order from the smallest to the largest. Just as a phoneme is a minimal, distinctive unit in the sound system of a language, a morpheme is a minimal, meaningful unit in the grammatical system of a language. The word **unhappy** consists of two morphemes **un-** and **happy**. Similarly, the word **un-grate-ful-ness** consists of four morphemes separated here by hyphens while the word *un-accept-able* consists of three morphemes.

Morphemes combine to form words. A *word* is the principal unit of lexicography, and each word finds a separate entry in the dictionary. Any group of words, which is grammatically equivalent to a single word and which does not have its own subject and predicate, is called a **phrase**. Here are some phrases: in a jiffy, the natives of South Africa, at one time or the other, in view of the shortage of petrol, etc. **A clause**, in contrast, has its own subject and predicate and is a part of a larger sentence, e.g.

If I go to Bombay, I shall bring a camera for you.

Subordinate clause Principal clause

A sentence is defined as a group of words that make sense. It is the largest unit of grammatical description and is an independent linguistic form.

Language, as we have said earlier, is an extremely complex phenomenon. The job of a grammarian is to study these complexities, try to find patterns in these complexities and, as far as possible, simplify them and explain them. It is a stupendous task which is impossible to fulfil but grammarians or students of language have, since time immemorial, been making an honest effort in that direction. There is no doubt that they have partially succeeded, but the successes achieved by various linguists in the case of various languages have proved beyond doubt that the labour put in is worth it and has not gone waste. The last word on grammar will, perhaps, never be said.

6.2 FUNCTIONS AND CATEGORIES

Ever since any serious studies in language were made, linguists, right from Plato and Aristotle, have been trying to divide words into several categories, popularly known as parts of speech. This, in fact, is the case with any scientific description that has its own set of technical terms. English grammar is also a scientific study and has, therefore, its own terms. Important categories or categorical labels in English, for example, are nouns, verbs, adjectives, adverbs, pronouns, prepositions, articles, conjunctions, ordinals, and quantifiers. Different linguists including Plato, Aristotle, Dionysius Thrax, and several later linguists have been giving their own lists of these categories, but everybody agrees that words can be divided into certain separate groups.

Some linguists group the words into two broad divisions: **full** words and **empty** words. **Full** words are also named by some as **form classes*** while **empty** words are named by some as **structure classes**. According to these linguists, full words are those words which have a high meaning value (nouns, verbs, adjectives, adverbs), e.g. chair, brandy, affection, play, nice, and quickly. Such words form the main body or the skeleton of the language. The list of such words is quite large and is open-ended as more and more words continue to be added to it every day.

Empty words, on the other hand, have a low meaning value or have no meaning at all. Their role in the language is that of grammatical linkers or markers of grammatical relationships. Such words include prepositions, conjunctions, articles, auxiliaries, etc. Their membership is small and closed. While the form of words belonging to the full words category changes so often in different sentences, the form of words belonging to the structure classes category remains the same.

Some linguists divide words into two classes:

- **Open class**
- **Closed class**

Words belonging to open class are those generally classified as nouns (e.g. pen, book, boy, brandy), verbs (e.g. cry, believe, become, appear), adjectives (e.g. good, painful, charming, tall) or adverbs (e.g. here, now, yesterday, calmly, soundly). These words are said to belong to the open class because more and more words continue to be added to this class. One can always coin new words to add to the existing stock of words in this group. Thus the membership of this group is open ended. English vocabulary is continually being extended by new words belonging to this group.

The closed class, on the other hand, has a fixed number of words in it. No new words are added to it. The closed class includes words generally classified as Determiners (e.g. a, an, the, some, any, this), Pronouns (e.g. I, me, you), Prepositions (e.g. in, at, on, upon, near), Conjunctions (e.g. and, or, but, when, because) and Modals (e.g. will, shall, can).

***Form classes** are also termed by some as **content words** or **lexical items**.

6.3 TRADITIONAL DEFINITIONS

Traditional grammarians tried to give meaning-based or notional definitions to these classes. These definitions were, in several ways, misleading. Here are a few examples from the English language. A **noun** was traditionally defined as the name of a place, person or thing. Now this definition fails to describe words like love, folly, suffering, army, etc. How about the word **yellow**? Is it not the name of a colour? But to which category does this word belong in the expression 'the yellow daffodils'? Similarly, the traditional definition of **verb** as a word that denotes action or process leads us nowhere. It fails to explain words like **construction**, **destruction**, etc. Do these words not stand for action or process? Still they are not verbs. Why not, therefore, define these categories (e.g. nouns, verbs) in terms of some characteristics? These characteristics too may not prove foolproof, yet taken as collective properties, these will certainly make it easier to identify one category from the other. Some of the notable characteristics of *nouns* are:

1. They form plurals by taking—e(s), e.g. tables, books (not nices, verys, lovelys, playeds).
2. They take possessive case, e.g. John's, ship's.
3. They can be typically preceded by articles, e.g. a girl, the beauty, the destruction, an inkpot.
4. Their form ends in a noun forming derivational suffix, e.g. ity (as in **ability**), -ness (as in **goodness**), -ism (as **in hooliganism**), -hood (as in **boyhood**), -ice (as in **cowardice**), -ship (as in **friendship**), -or (as in **narrator**).

All these characteristics or tests are not foolproof and they do admit of exceptions here and there. They can, however, be safely taken as collective properties of nouns. Similarly, verbs are traditionally defined as words that denote action or process. This definition too is not satisfactory as it fails to explain words like **beautification and destruction**, which certainly involve a lot of action. *Verbs* can be better described in terms of their grammatical characteristics, e.g.

(a) Verbs take the past or the past participle forms, e.g. take, took, taken.

(b) Verbs can be preceded by a noun and in many cases followed by a noun, e.g. Ram killed Ravana.

(c) Each verb has **three** or **more** of the following inflectional forms:

1	2	3	4	5
Verb	*Third person singular*	*Present participle*	*Past*	*Past participle*
Write	Writes	Writing	Wrote	Written
Sing	Sings	Singing	Sang	Sung
Cut	Cuts	Cutting	Cut	Cut

Similarly, it may be concluded that category labels like adjectives and adverbs too should be studied in terms of their characteristics, functions or properties.

6.31 Positional Classes

Apart from **form classes**, words may also be divided into **positional classes**. There are four main positional classes: **nominal**, **verbal**, **adjectival** and **adverbial**. Membership of words in these classes is determined by position or word order.

Here is an example:

All of us enjoyed the...

The blank here is a noun position. Any item that occupies the slot can be labelled a **nominal**. Some possible choices for the slot would be: movie, show, game, programme, art, performance, dance, drink, etc. Each of these choices is a **nominal**, though not necessarily a **noun.** Here is a set of sentences where the blank positions are characteristically the habitation of **verbals**.

We .... the game.
I .... a letter.
Your movement .... suspicion.
She .... nicely.

Adjectivals occupy a position as follows:

1. Between the determiner and the noun.
   That **plentiful** crop.
   An **inside** story.
   A **senior** teacher.
   That **college** insignia.
2. As a complement after the verb **be:**
   She is **nice.**
   The boys are **nasty**.
   The party was **enjoyable**.
3. As a complement after the **linking verb:**
   She appears **sensible.**
   He grew **sleepy.**
   The soup tasted **delicious**.
   We felt **weary.**
4. After the noun (post-nominal position).
   God **almighty** loves all.
   We have been worshipping God since time **immemorial.**
   The floor **below** is rented.
   A fire, **red** and **yellow**, was raging all over the area.

The positional class, adverbials, too occupy various positions in different sentences. It is, however, difficult to delimit their position without creating enormous complications.

Here is an example:

You will go to sleep **soon.**
Soon you will go to sleep.
You will **soon** go to sleep.
You will make your next move **skilfully.**
Skilfully you will make your next move.
You will **skilfully** make your next move.

6.4 EMPTY WORDS

Empty words or structure classes belong to categories whose membership is limited. It is, therefore, better to list them rather than going to traditional definitions. Amongst the structure classes are pronouns, prepositions, articles, ordinals (e.g. first, third, last), quantifiers, demonstratives (e.g. this, that, these, those), conjunctions, auxiliaries (modal as well as non-modal).

6.5 FUNCTIONAL LABELS

Amongst the functional labels are the words that give us an idea of the function of a particular word/phrase in the structure of the sentence. These labels include terms such as **subject, object, subject complement, and object complement.**

Any single sentence may have **essential** or **nuclear** part in it and some **marginal** elements (or **adjuncts**) that could be safely left out without destroying the essential sentence. Look at the following example:

[Mahatma Gandhi was shot dead] inside the Birla House building.

The part of the sentence inside the box is the essential or nuclear part of the sentence while the remaining part without which the sentence can still stand by itself is called the **adjunct**. In the following examples, the nuclear parts have been enclosed within rectangular brackets.

[He was sleeping] in his chair.

[I told him to leave] immediately.

A group of words that appears as adjunct in one sentence may be a nuclear part in another sentence, e.g.

He was **in his chair.**

I live **inside the Birla House building.**

It may once again be said that it may be **inaccurate** even to define terms such as 'subject', 'object', 'subject complement', and 'object complement' as the traditional grammarians have done. It would, however, be advisable to label a few sentences to give an idea of what these labels stand for.

(i) She	received	me	nicely	
Subject	Verb	Object	Adverb	(S–V–O–A)
(ii) She	taught	us	English.	
S	V	O	O	(S–V–O_I–O_D)
		Ind.	Dir.	

If the direct and indirect objects exchange places, the indirect object always takes a preposition in front of it, e.g.

She taught English **to** us.

(iii) He	became	minister.		
Subject	Verb	Complement		(S–V–C)
(iv) Ram	hit	a six	yesterday.	
Subject	Verb	Object	Adjunct	(S–V–O–A)
(v) The teacher	made	him	monitor.	
Subject	Verb	Object	Obj. complement	(S–V–O–OC)
(vi) The king	left	him	a broken man.	
Subject	Verb	Object	Sub. complement	(S–V–O–SC)

All this exercise is only meant to convey that the classification of words in a language is, no doubt, important, even necessary but one may not be guided solely by traditional meaning-based or notional definitions. In the course of the use of language, a user automatically comes to gain a sort of intuitive knowledge of the categories and functions of different words/phrases in his language.

SUMMARY

It is very difficult to define the term **grammar**. Everybody, however, intuitively knows what grammar is. The moment a person distinguishes between a sentence and a non-sentence, he is displaying his knowledge of grammar of the language. Grammar is an attempt to discover patterns in language structure, an attempt to classify words and sentences and then to deduce certain 'rules'. Grammar, being a scientific study, is *descriptive*, not prescriptive.

Grammar is said to operate between phonology and semantics. It studies the way in which words or morphemes join to form meaningful sentences. A study of grammar includes the study of five fundamental units of grammatical structure, viz. morpheme, word, phrase, clause and sentence.

Ever since the start of any serious studies in grammar, linguists have been trying to divide words into several categories, popularly known as **parts of speech.** Some linguists group words into two broad divisions: **full** words and **empty** words, while others divide these into **open** and **closed** classes.

Traditional grammarians tried to give **meaning-based** or **notional** definitions to various categories of words. These definitions were found to be unsatisfactory.

Later linguists, therefore, described the categories in terms of the characteristics of each category. Functional labels were also suggested for words/parts of sentence in a particular sentence. Everybody, however, agrees that the last word on grammar can never be said. It continues to grow with the growth of language every day.

COMPREHENSION QUESTIONS

1. What do you understand by the term **Grammar**?
2. Write a short note on the fundamental units of grammatical structure.
3. Distinguish between:
   (a) Functional labels and category labels
   (b) Open and closed classes
   (c) Form and structure class words
   (d) Empty and full words.
4. What do you understand by the term **parts of speech**? How do you find the traditional definitions of some parts of speech insufficient?
5. Write **True/False** against each of the following statements:
   (a) Grammar of a language is a book of rules pertaining to that particular language.
   (b) Language has no grammar.
   (c) A user of a language has the intuitive knowledge of the grammar of that language even though he may not have had a formal training in grammar.
   (d) **Nouns, Verbs** and **Adjectives** belong to the closed classes of words.

CHAPTER 7

Morphology and Word Formation

7.1 DEFINITION

According to the traditional linguistic theories, grammatical description largely operates on two important units: the **word** and the **sentence**. These two units form the basis of different writing systems in various languages of the world. This section is intended to examine the term **word** and the smaller elements that constitute words. A word is a single unit of language, which means something and can be spoken or written. The English word **unkind** is made up of two smaller units: **un** and **kind**. These are minimal units that cannot be further sub-divided into meaningful units. Such minimal, meaningful units of grammatical description are generally referred to as morphemes (already briefly introduced in Chapter 6). A morpheme is a short segment of language that meets three criteria:

1. It is a word or a part of a word that has meaning.
2. It cannot be divided into smaller meaningful parts without violation of its meaning or without meaningless remainders.
3. It recurs in differing verbal environments with a relatively stable meaning.

The word **unlikely** has three morphemes while the word **carpet** is a single morpheme. The words **car** and **pet** are independent morphemes in themselves, but the word **carpet** has nothing to do with the meanings of **car** and **pet. Carpet** is a minimal meaningful unit by itself. Again, the word **garbage** is a single morpheme while the words **garb** and **age** are independent morphemes by themselves. A systematic study of morphemes or how morphemes join to form words is known as **morphology**.

The definition of the morpheme may not be completely unassailable as will be evident from the discussion that follows, but it is certainly a very satisfying definition applicable to a majority of words in any language. The English word **unassailable** is made up of three morphemes, **un, assail, able,** each one of which has a particular meaning distribution and a particular phonological form or shape.

7.2 SEGMENTATION

A large number of such words as can be divided into segments are said to be determinate with respect to segmentation.

EXAMPLES

boys	boy-s	unable	un-able
playing	play-ing	knowingly	know-ing-ly
passed	pass-ed	watches	watch-es

But there are several words which can either not be segmented (indeterminate) at all or are only partially determinate with respect to segmentation.

EXAMPLES

men, children, mice, sheep, went, took, broke,
sang, brought, better, best, worse, worst.

The problems of segmentation in all such words may vary in kind as well as in degree. This presents a serious problem. Although **better** and **went** stand in the same grammatical relationship with **good** and **go** as **higher** and **played** have with **high** and **play**, yet the words **better** and **went** cannot be segmented into parts (as **higher** and **played**) as per the given definition of the term morpheme. Since we know that **better** has the same grammatical function vis-a-vis **good** as **taller** has vis-a-vis **tall**, we can express the relationship as a proportion of grammatical (or distributional) equivalence:

good : better : best :: tall : taller : tallest

Good and **tall** are both adjectives and the expression **better** and **taller** are grammatically alike in the sense that they both express only the comparative degree of the adjective. Similarly, **best** and **tallest** too are alike as they express the superlative degree of the adjective. Now suppose, on an analogy from algebra, we resolve each of the six words given above into factors/components, the word **good** being denoted by the factor a, tall by b, the positive, comparative and superlative functions being marked by factors x, y and z respectively, the above equivalence can be rewritten as

ax : ay : az :: bx : by : bz

All the three words on the left-hand side have the component *a* (i.e. good) in them and those on the right-hand side have the component **b** (i.e. tall) in them. Components x, y and z stand to mark the positive, comparative and superlative degrees of the adjectives in question. All these components, or distributional factors of words are morphemes. Thus a morpheme may not necessarily be a part or segment of a word, it may merely have a **factorial** role as indicated above. When a word is segmented into parts, the segments are referred to as 'morphs'. The word **happier** thus consists of two morphs which can be orthographically written as **happy** and **er** (conventions of English orthography allowing a change of y into i). In phonological transcription, the two morphs can be represented as /hæpɪ/ and /ə/. Each morph thus represents (or is the exponent or factor of) a particular morpheme.

The terms 'morpheme' and 'morph' are thus comparable to the terms 'form' and 'substance' given by F. de Saussure. The morpheme is an element of form which may be represented directly by phonological (or orthographical) segments with a particular 'shape' (i.e. by morphs). It is customary to represent morphemes between braces. For example, the word **went** (phonologically /went/) which cannot be segmented into morphs, represents the combination of two morphemes: *go* and *past*.

Sometimes, a particular morpheme may be represented not by the same morph but by different morphs in different environments. Such different representations of a morpheme are called *allomorphs*.

The plural morpheme in English (which combines with a noun morpheme to form a plural) is represented by three allomorphs /s/, /z/ and /ɪz/ in different environments (which are phonologically conditioned).

Plural morpheme

Allomorphs

Plural morpheme {e(s)} —

→/ɪz/ in the case of words ending in /s/, /z/, /ʃ/, /ʒ/, /tʃ/, /dʒ/
e.g. buses /bʌsɪz/, vases /vɑ: zɪz/, bushes / b ʊ ʃ ɪz/, rouges /ru : ʒɪz/, churches /tʃʒ : tʃɪz/ judges/, /dʒʌdʒɪz/

→/s/ in the case of words ending in a voiceless consonant (other than ʃ, s, tʃ): cats /kæts/, caps /kæps/

→/z/ in the case of words ending in voiced sounds (other than / z, ʒ, dʒ/):
boys: bɔɪz/, bags /bægz/

Similarly, the present tense morpheme {–e(s)} has three allomorphs /s/, /z/ and /ɪz/, e.g. packs /pæks/, digs /digz/, washes /wɒʃɪz/. The past tense morpheme of English, {–e(d)} has also three different (phonologically conditioned) allomorphs /t/, /d/ and /ɪd/. The rule that governs these allomorphs is as follows:

Past morpheme

Past morpheme {e(d)} —

→/t/ after morphs ending in voiceless sounds (except /t/)
booked /bʊkt/, pushed /pʊʃt/

→/d/ after morphs ending in voiced sounds (except /d/).
loved /lʌvd/, bagged /bægd/

→/ɪd/ after morphs ending in /t/ and /d/ wanted /wɒntɪd/ wedded / wedɪd/

The relationship between the terms **morph**, **allomorph** and **morpheme** is similar to that between **phone**, **allophone** and **phoneme**. The term 'morph' means shape. Any minimal phonetic form that has meaning is a morph. Thus /bʌs/, /ɪz/, /bʊʃ/, /ɪz/, /kæp/, /s/, /bɔɪ/, /z/ are all morphs. Those morphs which belong to the same morpheme are called **allomorphs** of that morpheme. Thus, /s/, /z/ and /ɪz/

are allomorphs of the plural morpheme {e(s)}. This is just like a phoneme which is a minimal, distinctive unit in the sound system of a language. A phoneme may sometimes occur in more than one phonetic form called allophones. These phonetic forms have considerable phonetic similarity between them, and their phonological function is the same. They, however, never occur in the same phonetic environment and are said to be in complementary distribution. Similarly, allomorphs are also in complementary distribution. The phonemes /p/, /t/ and /k/, for example, have two phonetic forms each, i.e. [p] and [ph], [t] and [t^h], [k] and [k^h]. Here, [p] and [ph] are the allophones of the phoneme /p/. All the speech sounds (phonemes as well as allophones) are called **phones**.

It may be noted that in some languages words can generally be segmented into parts (morphs) while this is not so in others. Similarly, there are languages in which the morph tends to represent a single minimal grammatical unit (a morpheme) while there are others in which this is not so. Allomorphs too exist in some languages only.

We can now clearly bring out both the grammatical similarity and the formational difference between such words as **brought** and **played**, or **worse** and **taller**. Both the regular and the irregular forms can be handled alike:

brought = {bring} + {ed}; played = {play} + {ed}

worse = {bad} + {er}; taller {tall} + {er}, etc.

7.3 FREE AND BOUND MORPHEMES

In words such as **unhappy**, **disregarded**, **boyhood**, etc., morphemes such as **happy**, **regard** and **boy** can stand on their own as independent words. Such morphemes are called *free morphemes*. On the other hand, morphemes like un-, dis-, -ed, –hood, etc., cannot stand on their own as independent words. They are always attached to a free morpheme or a free form. Such morphemes are called 'bound morphemes'. Morphemes such as dis-, un-, -ed, -hood are also called affixes. The form to which an affix is attached is called a base. Here is a tree diagram showing the morphological analysis of the word **unknowingly**:

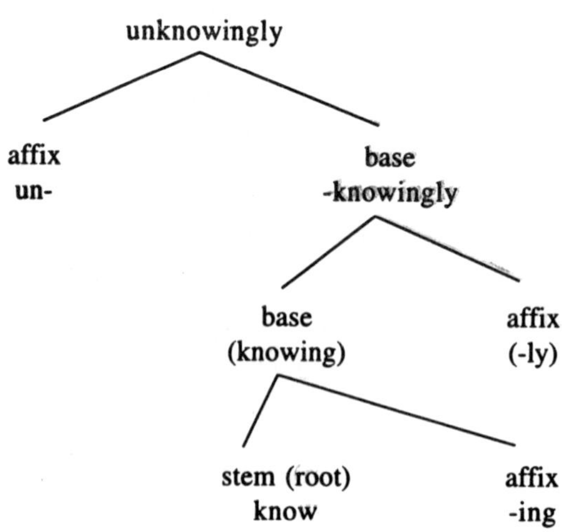

The stem that cannot be further split up is also called the **root**.

Affixes may be divided into prefixes (which appear at the beginning of the base) and suffixes (which appear at the end of the base). Consider the following sets:

Set A				**Set B**	
	Prefix	*Base*		*Base*	*Suffix*
unhappy	un-	happy	friendship	friend	-ship
immobile	im-	mobile	boyhood	boy	-hood
enable	en-	able	boys	boy	-s
illegal	il-	legal	nicely	nice	-ly

(Note that when cited in isolation, a prefix has a hyphen after it while a suffix has a hyphen before it.)

On another dimension, affixes are classified as inflectional affixes and derivational affixes. Inflection is a change made in the form of a word to express its relation to other words in the sentence. Derivation, on the other hand, is the process by which new words are formed from existing words. Derivation is class-maintaining if the original word and the new word belong to the same class (e.g. **boy** and **boyhood**, both nouns, **play** and **replay**, both verbs) and is class-changing if the two words belong to different categories (e.g. **able** and **enable**: verb from adjective; **season** and **seasonal**: adjective from noun; **sing** and **singer**: noun from verb).

Properties of the Inflectional suffixes:

(i) Inflectional suffixes do not change the class of the word, e.g.

slide	slides	(both verbs)
hot	hotter	(both adjectives)
girl	girls	(both nouns)
play	playing	(both verbs)

(ii) They come last in a word and appear only as suffixes. (It may be noted that derivational affixes can be prefixes as well as suffixes).

(iii) They do not pile up (only one ends a word), e.g. pens, higher, laughing, written.

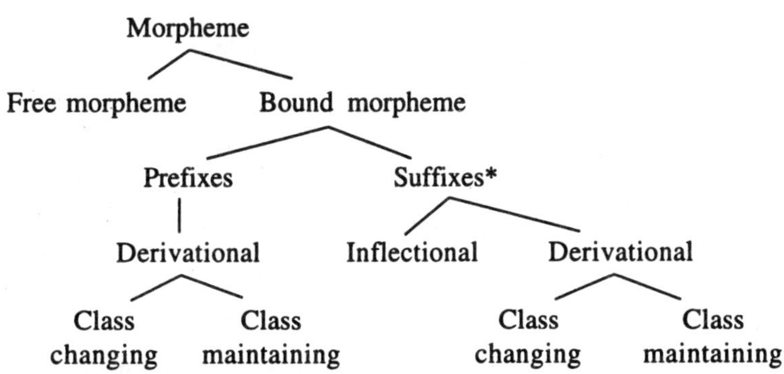

*Words like **went** are taken to be = go + ed (see Section 6.1).

(iv) Also, inflectional suffixes go with all stems of a given part of speech, e.g.

Verbs		*Adjectives*		*Nouns*	
go	goes	cold	colder	boy	boys
play	plays	tall	taller	table	tables
see	sees	high	higher	bench	benches

The following diagram summarises all the statements made above (applicable to English language only):

7.4 MORPHOLOGICAL ANALYSIS OF A FEW WORDS

(i)

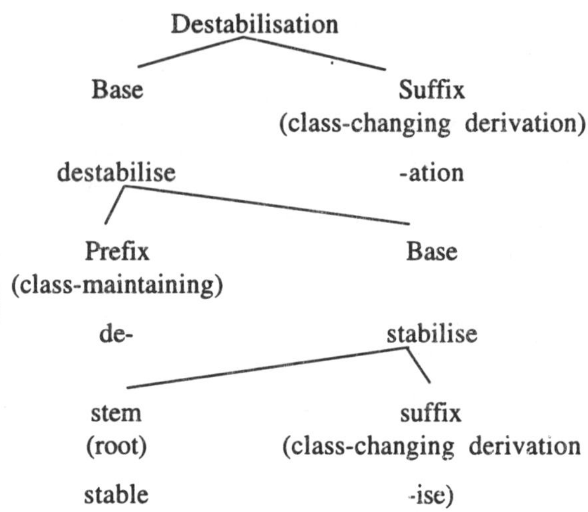

(ii)

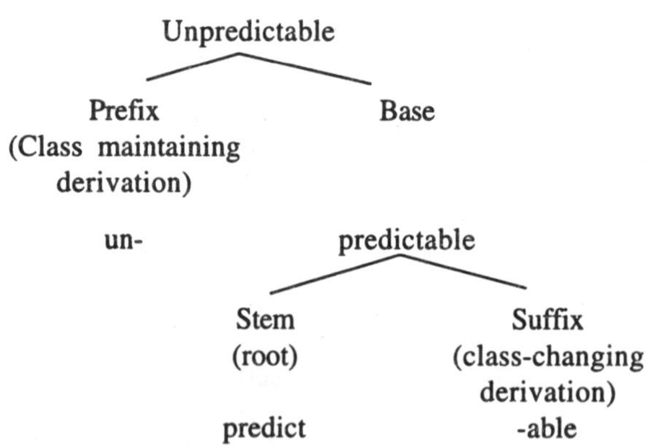

7.5 STRUCTURE OF WORDS*

Considered from the point of view of their morpheme constituents, there are mainly three types of words: Simple words, complex words and compound words.

---

* As a corollary, it may be noted that the morphological analysis of words leads one to the **formation** of new words. For details, refer Chapter 7.

(i) *Simple words.* They consist of a single free morpheme followed, or not, by an inflectional suffix, e.g. play, plays, stronger.

(ii) *Complex words.* They consist of a base and a derivational affix, e.g. goodness, enable, boyhood, determination.

(iii)

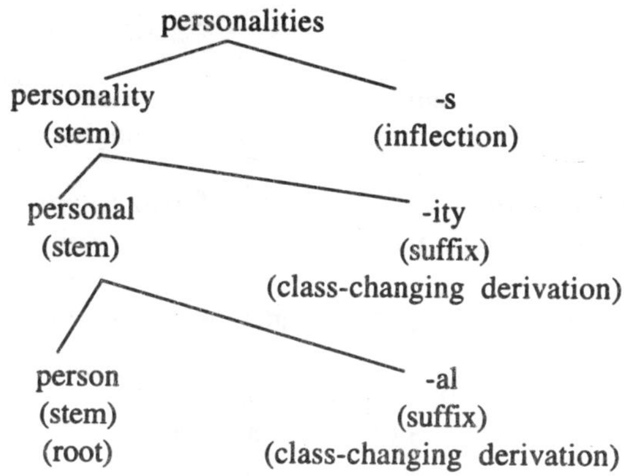

(iv)

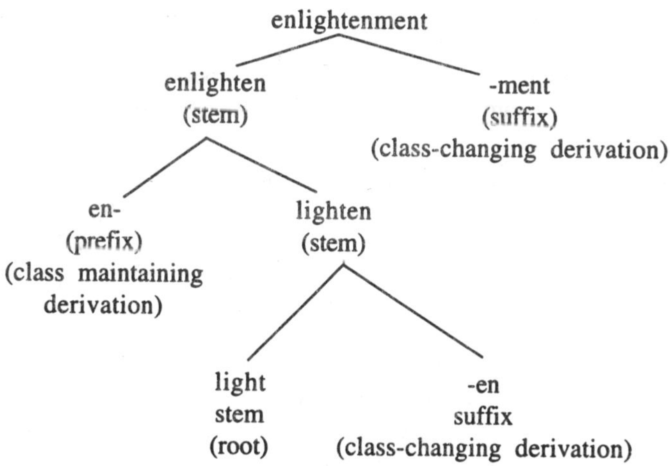

(v)

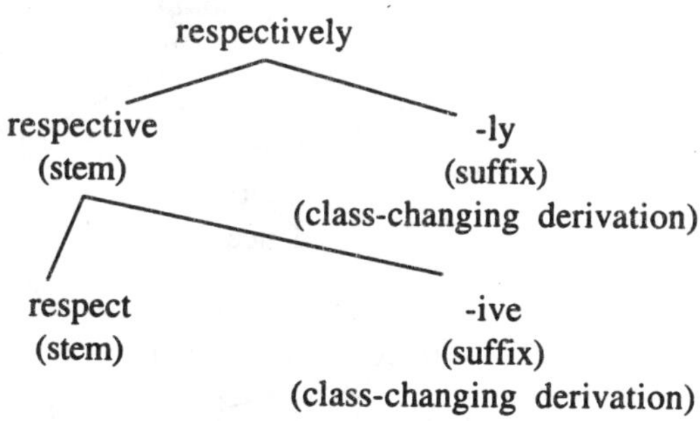

(vi)

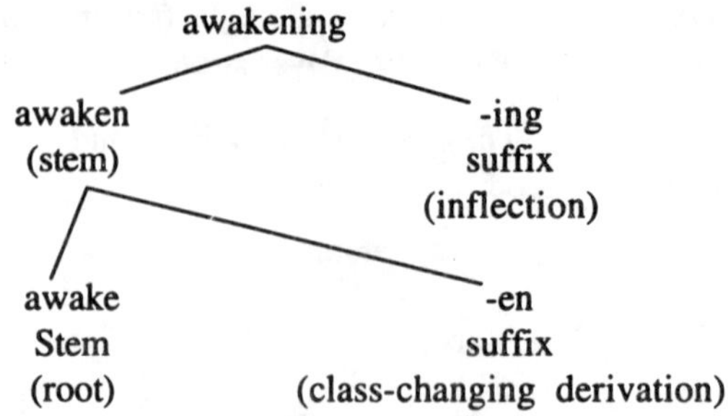

(iii) ***Compound words.*** They consist of two (or more) free stems which are independent words by themselves, e.g. over-ripe, happy-go-lucky, elevator-operator.

A morphological analysis of a few more words will further clarify the position:

(i)

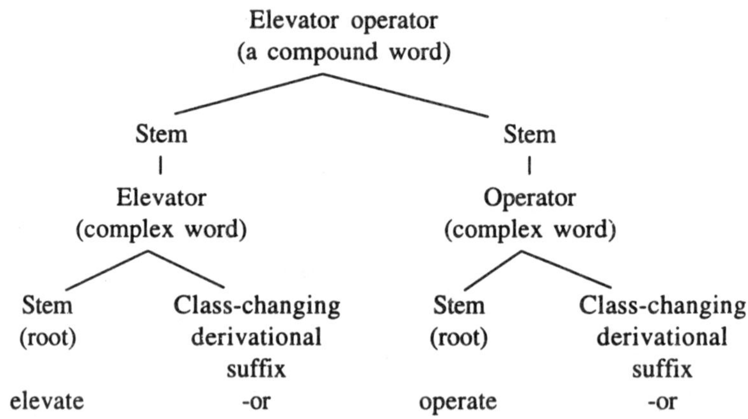

(ii)

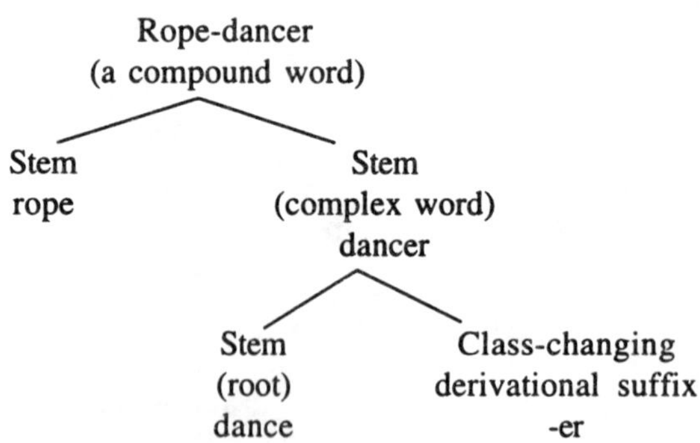

(iii)

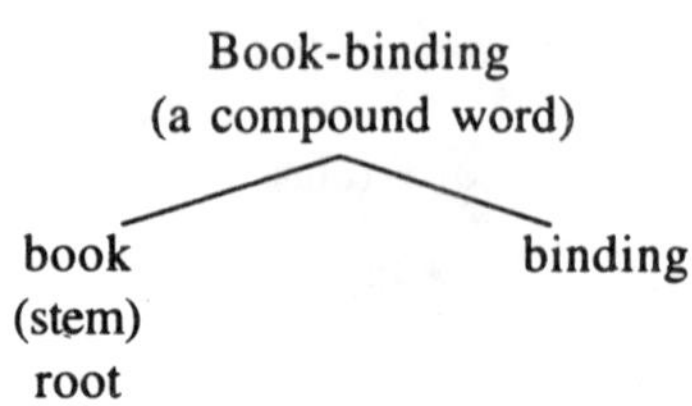

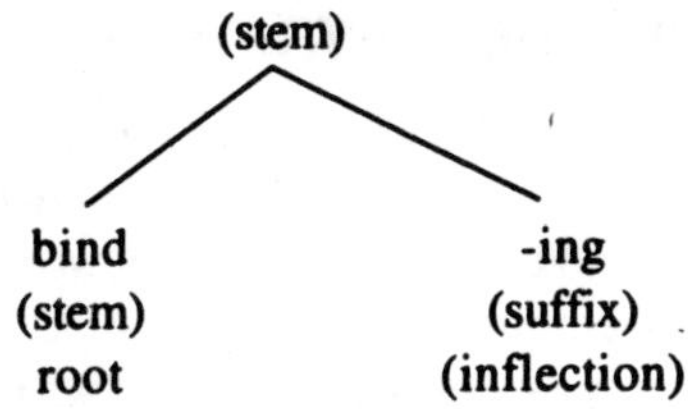
(stem)
bind
(stem)
root
-ing
(suffix)
(inflection)

(iv)

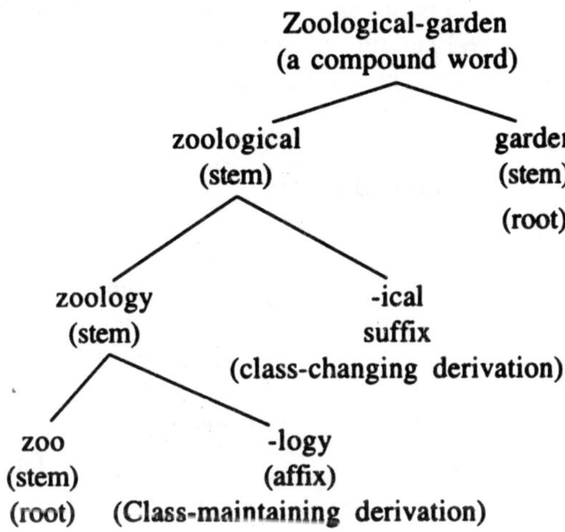
Zoological-garden
(a compound word)
zoological
(stem)
garden
(stem)
(root)
zoology
(stem)
-ical
suffix
(class-changing derivation)
zoo
(stem)
(root)
-logy
(affix)
(Class-maintaining derivation)

(v)

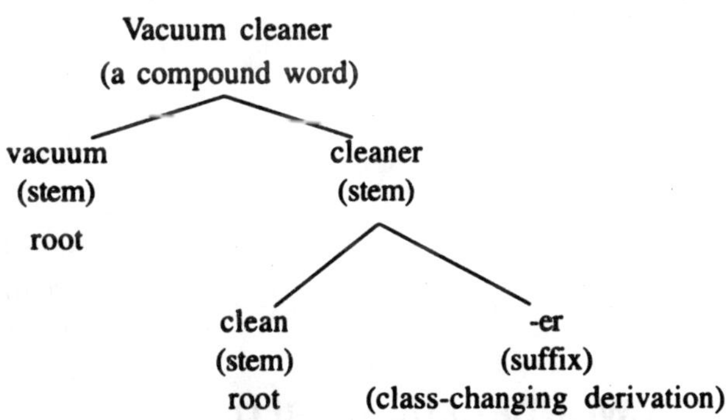
Vacuum cleaner
(a compound word)
vacuum
(stem)
root
cleaner
(stem)
clean
(stem)
root
-er
(suffix)
(class-changing derivation)

(vi)

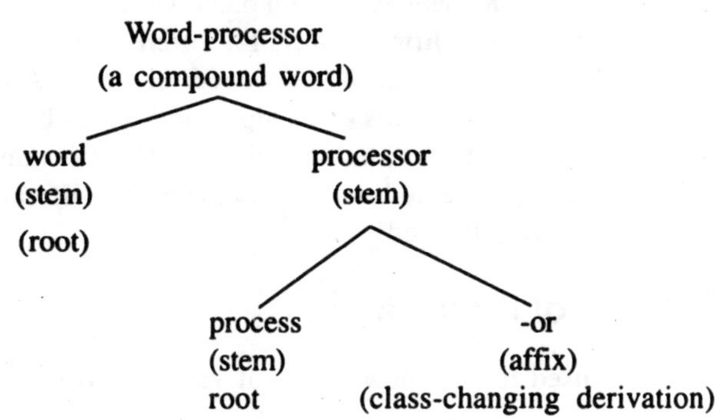
Word-processor
(a compound word)
word
(stem)
(root)
processor
(stem)
process
(stem)
root
-or
(affix)
(class-changing derivation)

7.6 VARIOUS WAYS OF WORD FORMATION

The users of a language have to be conversant with the myriad ways in which words are formed. A simple word like **happiness**, for example, is formed by adding the suffix **-ness** to the base word **happy**. While happy is an adjective, happiness is a noun. The word 'happiness' has thus been derived from the word 'happy'. This most important method of word formation is known as **affixation,** i.e. by adding a prefix or a suffix to a **base** called **stem**. Any form to which an affix (either prefix or suffix) is added is called a stem. A stem is called a root when all affixes are removed from it (see Examples (a) and (b) below). Every stem can, however, be a base. The stem cannot be further broken up into two separate morphemes. Here are two examples:

(a)

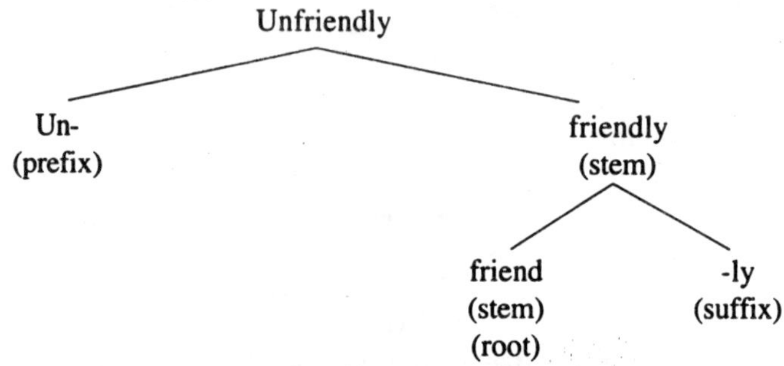

(b)

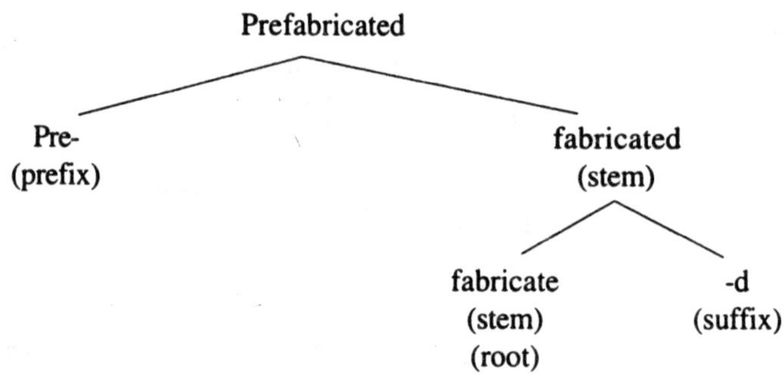

7.7 A WONDERFUL WORLD

Apart from affixation, there are several other ways in which new words are formed. Also, words are used in different ways for different meanings or connotations. The world of words in any language is a wonderful world. A user of a language who masters the art of using words or manipulating words becomes a wizard with the language and proves to be a master in the skill of communication. It would be quite pertinent, therefore, to briefly list some of the different ways in which words are formed or skilfully used.

7.71 Use of Prefixes

Prefixes are used to coin new words of various types:

(a) Negative prefixes

Prefix	Base word	New word
im-	possible/mortal	impossible/immortal
in-	evitable	inevitable
	sensitive	insensitive
un-	stable	unstable
	like	unlike
a-	theist	atheist
	moral	amoral
non-	entity	non-entity
	violence	non-violence
dis-	passionate	dispassionate
	service	disservice
il-	logical	illogical
	limitable	illimitable
ir-	rational	irrational
	relevant	irrelevant
de-	frost	defrost
	forestation	deforestation
mis-	interpret	misinterpret
	represent	misrepresent
pseudo-	secular	pseudosecular
	religious	pseudoreligious

(b) Prefixes of number

mono-	syllabic	monosyllabic
	logue	monologue
uni-	lateral	unilateral
	cellular	unicellular
bi-	lingual	bilingual
	lateral	bilateral
di-	pole	dipole
	ode (electrode)	diode
	urnal	diurnal
tri-	weekly	triweekly
	angle	triangle
tetra-	cyclic	tetracyclic
multi/poly-	syllabic	polysyllabic
	racial	multiracial
	pronged	multipronged
	lingual	multilingual

(c) Prefixes of time and order

re-	evaluate	re-evaluate
	examine	re-examine

Prefix	Base word	New word
ante-	chamber	antechamber
fore-	knowledge	fore-knowledge
	tell	foretell
pre-	natal	prenatal
	mature	premature
post-	war	post-war
	dated	post-dated
ex-	MLA	ex-MLA
	principal	ex-principal
super-	structure	superstructure
	fine	superfine

(d) Prefixes of location

sub-	way	subway
	terranean	subterranean
	marine	submarine
Inter-/intra-	national	international
	class	interclass
	group	intragroup
	departmental	intra-departmental
trans-	plant	transplant
	migration	transmigration

(e) Prefixes of degree or size

super-	man	superman
	natural	supernatural
out-	run	outrun
	live	outlive
under-	state	understate
	cooked	undercooked
hyper-	active	hyperactive
	critical	hypercritical
ultra-	modern	ultramodern
	simple	ultrasimple
mini- (midi-/maxi-)	bus	minibus
	skirt	miniskirt
over-	active	overactive
	smart	oversmart
sub-	human	subhuman
	zero	subzero
	standard	substandard
arch-	bishop	archbishop
	angel	archangel

(f) Prefixes of attitude

pro-	congress	pro-congress
	democracy	pro-democracy
anti-	hindu	anti-hindu
	social	anti-social
co-	operate	cooperate
	sponsor	cosponsor
counter-	act	counteract
	proposal	counterproposal

(g) Other prefixes

auto-	biography	autobiography
	start	autostart
neo-	rich	neorich
	classical	neoclassical
semi-	circle	semicircle
	nude	seminude
pan-	Indian	pan-Indian

(h) Class-changing prefixes

Here are examples of some prefixes that change the class to which a word belongs:

Prefix	Word	Class	New word	Class
be-	head	noun	behead	verb
	friend	noun	befriend	verb
en-	able	adjective	enable	verb
	trust	noun	entrust	verb
a-	float	verb	afloat	adjective
	head	noun	ahead	adjective
de-	form	noun	deform	verb
	frost	noun	defrost	verb

7.72 Use of Suffixes

The suffixes may be broadly divided into two categories: class-maintaining and class-changing. Here are a few examples:

(a) Class-maintaining suffixes

Suffix	Word	Class	New word	Class
-ship	friend	noun	friendship	noun
-hood	boy	noun	boyhood	noun
ite	hindu	adjective	hinduite	adjective
-er	London	noun	Londoner	noun
ess-	tiger	noun	tigress	noun

-dom	king	noun	kingdom	noun
-ery	machine	noun	machinery	noun

(b) Class-changing suffixes

(i) Noun to adjective

-ian	India	noun	Indian	adjective
-ese	China	noun	Chinese	adjective
-ful	beauty	noun	beautiful	adjective
-less	harm	noun	harmless	adjective
-ly	friend	noun	friendly	adjective
-like	child	noun	childlike	adjective
-ish	child	noun	childish	adjective
-al	accident	noun	accidental	adjective
-ous	virtue	noun	virtuous	adjective

(ii) Adjectives to noun

-ity	able	adjective	ability	noun
-ness	happy	adjective	happiness	noun
-ry	brave	adjective	bravery	noun

(iii) Nouns to verbs

-ify	fort	noun	fortify	verb
-en	length	noun	lengthen	verb
-le	top	noun	topple	verb

(iv) Verbs to nouns

-er	drive	verb	driver	noun
-ment	govern	verb	government	noun
-age	drain	verb	drainage	noun
-ant	pollute	verb	pollutant	noun
-ee	pay	verb	payee	noun
-ation	condemn	verb	condemnation	noun
-al	withdraw	verb	withdrawal	noun
-or	act	verb	actor	noun

(v) Verbs to adverb

-ily	sleep	verb	sleepily	adverb
-fully	play	verb	playfully	adverb

(vi) Adjectives to adverbs

-ly	nice	adjective	nicely	adverb
-wards	back	adjective	backwards	adverb

7.73 Conversions

(a) Some words can be used as nouns, verbs, adverbs or adjectives without any change in the form of the word, without the addition of an affix or prefix. This process of derivation is called **conversion**. Here are some examples:

Light: Switch on the **light** (noun).
Light the lamp (verb).

Round: The earth is **round** like a ball (adjective).
The principal went on a **round** (noun).
You must **round** all the sharp corners (verb).

Back: He is carrying a bag on his **back** (noun).
You must **back** me up (verb).
The plane flew **back** in no time (adverb).
He left by the **back** door (adjective).

(b) Other types of conversion

(i) Please give me two **coffees**.
(An uncountable noun used as a countable noun)
(ii) This instrument is a **must** for you.
(A closed system word being used as a noun)
(iii) I do not like this **touch-me-not** policy.
(A phrase being used as an adjective)
(iv) I do not believe in any **ism** bothering the society today.
(A suffix being used as a noun)
(v) He is only **being** nice.
(Stative verb used as a dynamic verb)

(c) In some words of two syllables, change of accent from the first to the second syllable changes a noun/adjective to a verb:

Noun/Adjective	Verb
'conduct	con'duct
'subject	sub'ject
'object	ob'ject
'present	pre'sent
'contrast	con'trast

(d) There are some words, in which there is a change in the meanings of words if the final consonant is voiced (either by a change in spellings or without it); for example:

Word	Final sound	Word	Final sound
advice (n.)	/s/	advise (v.)	/z/
thief (n.)	/f/	thieve (v.)	/v/
house (n.)	/s/	house (v.)	/z/

7.74 Compound Formation

Compounds are formed by joining two or more bases. These bases are, in some cases, separated by a hyphen, while in other cases, the hyphen appears to have disappeared with the passage of time. There is no rule governing the presence or absence of the hyphen. Here are some examples of compound words:

(a) Noun + Noun

motor cycle	hair breadth
teargas	goldfish
girl-friend	television fan
bread-piece	block-head
fire-engine	pot-belley
paper-back	

(b) Noun + Adjective

trustworthy	beauty conscious
home sick	brickred
duty free	sea-green

(c) Adjective + Noun

paleface	yellow press
	red light
fathead	greenhorn

(d) Compounds with verbs/adverbials/verbal nouns

sight-seeing	man-eating
birth-control	heart-breaking
record-player	easy-going
brain-washing	baby-sitting
walking-stick	lip-read

7.75 Reduplication

Some words are formed out of two such elements as are almost alike. These elements may either be identical or only slightly different.

EXAMPLES

criss-cross	pooh-pooh	hush-hush
doodle-doo	kit-kat	see-saw
wishy-washy	tip-top	hurry-worry
trin-trin	hanky-panky	sing-song
walkie-talkie	humdrum	goody-goody

7.76 Clippings

Some words are used in shortened form by subtracting one or more syllables from a word. This shortening sometimes occurs at the beginning of a word, at the end of a word, or at both ends of a word.

EXAMPLES

Shortened word	Full word
photo	photograph
plane	aeroplane
pram	perambulator
bus	omnibus
flu	influenza
phone	telephone
hanky	handkerchief
maths	mathematics
lab	laboratory

7.77 Acronyms

An acronym is formed by joining together the initial letters (or sometimes a little larger parts) of other words and is pronounced as a word.

EXAMPLES

Acronyms	Full form
AIDS	Acquired Immuno Deficiency Syndrome
BASIC	Beginners All-purpose Symbolic Instruction Code (A computer language)
B2C	Business to Customer
LASER	Light Amplification by Simulated Emission of Radiation
UNICEF	United Nations International Children's Emergency Fund
UNESCO	United Nations Educational Scientific and Cultural Organisation

The difference between an **acronym** and an **abbreviation** is that the latter may be formed from the initial letters in a phrase on name and is read letter by letter, e.g. IBM, BA, M.Sc., AD, and so on, while the former is formed from the first letter of each word and is normally pronounced as a word e.g. LASER, BASIC.

7.78 Blends

Two words are sometimes clipped and the clippings joined to form a new word.

EXAMPLES

Brunch	*From*	breakfast and lunch
smog	*From*	smoke and fog
telecast	*From*	television and broadcast
motel	*From*	motorists and hotel

7.79 Borrowings

English (or any other language) generally borrows words from other languages with which it comes into contact. English continues to enrich its store of words by such borrowings.

EXAMPLES

Guru	*From*	Hindi
bazaar	*From*	Persian
Sheikh	*From*	Arabic
tycoon	*From*	Japanese
Dame	*From*	French

7.80 Inventions

New words have to be given to new inventions. Such words (as other words of the language) are arbitrary but in the course of time, they come to stay as a part of the language.

EXAMPLES

X-rays, laser, sputnik, astronaut.

7.81 Echoism

Some words are formed by the sounds that suggest their meaning.

EXAMPLES

clang, whisper, thunder, click, tick, lisp, murmur.

Language, as everybody knows, is dynamic. It continues to acquire new words with the passage of time. Some words also go on disappearing, as time passes, due to a variety of reasons. This confirms what we said earlier in Chapter 1 that language is open-ended and modifiable.

SUMMARY

A word may consist of a single morpheme or a number of morphemes. A morpheme is a minimal, meaningful unit in the grammatical system of a language. A systematic study of morphemes or how morphemes join to form words is known as morphology. A large number of words can be broken into segments. Such words are said to be **determinate** with respect to segmentation while some others (e.g. broke, better) are **indeterminate** with respect to segmentation. In the case of the words belonging to the latter type, it is conventional to use the term 'factor' for morphemes e.g. broke = {break} + {ed}.

Sometimes a particular morpheme may be represented not by the same morph but by different morphs in different phonetic environments. Such different representations of a morpheme are called allomorphs. The plural morpheme in English, for example, is represented by three different allomorphs,

/s/, /z/ and /ɪz/ in different environments.

Some morphemes can stand on their own as independent morphemes (e.g. **happy, regard, boy**). Such morphemes are called *free* morphemes. On the other hand, morphemes like, **-ed, un-**, which cannot stand on their own as independent words, are called *bound* morphemes. Bound morphemes are also called *affixes.* Affixes may be divided into prefixes or suffixes.

The users of a language have to be conversant with the myriad ways in which words are formed. The most important method of word formation is *affixation*, i.e. by adding a prefix or a suffix to a base word. Apart from affixation, there are several other methods by which new words are formed. Some of these methods are: compound formation (e.g. girl friend, fire engine, pot-belley), reduplication (e.g. kit-kat, pooh-pooh, ding-dong), use of clippings (e.g. photo, phone, plane), use of acronyms (e.g. AIDS, UNICEF), blend formation (e.g. brunch, smog, telecast), echoism (e.g. clang, tick), from new inventions (e.g. laser, sputnik) or from borrowings (e.g. sheikh, guru).

COMPREHENSION QUESTIONS

1. What is morphology? What do you understand by the term morpheme? How does it differ from a phoneme?
2. Give some examples of words which are (a) determinate and (b) indeterminate with respect to segmentation.
3. Define the terms 'morph', 'allomorph', 'morpheme'. Give examples.
4. Write a note on different allomorphs of the plural morpheme and the past morpheme in English.

5. What are free and bound morphemes? Give examples.
6. What are inflectional and derivational affixes? Explain with examples.
7. Give a morphological analysis of the following words:

Unknowingly	democratisation
unexplainable	fulfilment
elevator-operator	tight-rope-dancer

8. What are simple, complex and compound words? Explain with examples.
9. What are the different ways of word formation? Give examples.
10. What do you understand by affixation? Explain, giving copious examples.
11. Analyse the following words: unfriendly, unsurpassable, uncompromising, tight-rope-walker, preordained.
12. Distinguish class-changing suffixes from class-maintaining suffixes. Give examples.
13. Write a detailed note on the use of prefixes in the formation of words in English.
14. Some words in English can be used as belonging to different grammatical categories. Explain, with examples.
15. Change of accent can bring about a change in meaning. How? Give examples.
16. (a) Form verbs from: advice, thief, gait, fruit, able.
    (b) Form adjectives from: blood, work, play, society, humanity.
    (c) Form nouns from: hinder, democratic, operate, befriend, migrate.
17. Fill in the blanks:
    (a) **Smog** is made up of .... and ....
    (b) **UNICEF** is an acronym standing for ....
    (c) The word **plane** is the shortened form of .....
    (d) The word **subject** (n) becomes a .... if it is accented on the second syllable.
    (e) The common term used for both prefixes as well as suffixes is ....

CHAPTER 8

Basic Sentence Patterns

8.1 A BASIC SENTENCE

A **basic** (or a Kernel) sentence is the simplest form of sentence which is simple (not complex or compound), declarative and affirmative and is in the active voice. Such sentences can be broadly classified into five different patterns. Two of these patterns are **Intransitive** (using such verbs as do not take an object) while the other **three** are **transitive** (verbs that take an object). Given below are the detailed examples of all these types.

8.2 INTRANSITIVE PREDICATE PHRASE PATTERNS

8.21 Pattern I: Verbal Group only or Verbal Group (+ Adjunct)

Note: An Adjunct is a part of the sentence that can be taken out without breaking the structure of the sentence, e.g. Ramesh died yesterday at Ludhiana. If the words **yesterday** and **at Ludhiana** are removed, the sentence can still stand, but it cannot stand if the words **Ramesh** and/or **died** are removed. Such words (e.g. **yesterday, at Ludhiana**) form the adjunct while the remaining words form the **nuclear** part of the sentence.

I saw him	in the theatre.
(nuclear part)	(adjunct)
He is in the theatre	now.
(nuclear part)	(adjunct)

EXAMPLES (of sentences belonging to Pattern-I)*

(i)	He	passed away.	
	Sub.	VG	
(ii)	The teacher	shouted	at the top of his voice.
	Sub.	VG	Adjunct

---

*Abbreviations given represent:
Sub. = Subject, VG = Verbal group, Comp. = Complement, Obj. = Object, Dir./Indir. = Direct/Indirect, Adv. = Adverbial, Prep. phr. = Prepositional phrase NP = Noun phrase, Adj. phr. = Adjective phrase, Pred. phr. = Predicate phrase.

(iii)	The car	turned	into a narrow lane.	
	Sub.	VG	Adjunct	
(iv)	They	will write	about it	to the governor.
	Sub.	VG	Adjunct	Adjunct
(v)	The meeting	broke up	in a huff.	
	Sub.	VG	Adjunct	

8.22 Pattern II: Verbal Group + Complement (+ Adjunct)

The complement may be a noun phrase, an adverbial, a preposition phrase or an adjective phrase.

EXAMPLES

(i)	Rita	was	a damned witch.
	Sub.	VG	Complement (NP)
(ii)	Rita	was	in a fix.
		VG	Prep. phr.
(iii)	Rita	is	beautiful.
		VG	Adjective
(iv)	Rita	is	there.
		VG	Adverbial

MORE EXAMPLES

(i)	He	became	nasty	in the course of time.
		VG	Comp.	Adjunct
(ii)	He	appears	broken	
		VG	Comp.	

Contrast from: He appeared at the door step. Pattern I

He	appeared	at the door step. Pattern I
	VG	Adjunct

(iii)	The salad	tastes	delicious.	
		VG	Comp.	
(iv)	She	resembles	an ape.	
		VG	Comp.	
(v)	She	did not behave	herself	at the party.
		VG	Comp.	Adjunct
(vi)	The sky	got	dark.	
		VG	Comp.	
(vii)	Your mouth	smells	like a garbage box.	
		VG	Comp.	

It may be noted, as is evident from the examples given above, that all verbal groups cannot take all the four categories of complements, i.e. noun phrase, an adverbial, a preposition phrase or an adjective phrase. Depending upon the categories that verbal groups can take as complements, these verbal groups can be divided into six different categories:

(a) Be-type

(is, am, are, was, were, be, been, being)

In this case, the verbal group can take all the four categories as complements.

EXAMPLES

Rita	is VG	an interesting girl. NP
Rita	was VG	very nice. Adj. phr.
She	has been VG	in a fix. Prep. phr.
We	are VG	there. Adverbial

(b) Become type

Here, the verbal group can take a noun phrase and an adjective phrase as complements (not an adverbial or a preposition phrase).

EXAMPLES

He	became VG	a terrorist. NP	
She	became VG	powerful Adj. phr.	(one cannot say She became in Jalandhar or She became there)
He	got VG	nervous. Adj. phr.	
He turned out VG		a notorious criminal. Adj. phr.	
He appears VG		foolish. Adj. phr.	
He appears VG		a fool. NP	

(c) Smell-type

In this case, the verbal group can take an adjective phrase as a complement (not any of the other three).

EXAMPLES

The pudding	tastes VG	delicious. Adj. phr.
The soup	smells VG	horrible. Adj. phr.
The king	felt VG	helpless. Adj. phr.

(d) Have-type

In this case, the verbal group can take only the noun phrase as complements.

EXAMPLES

She	has VG	a pen. NP
Sita	resembles VG	her mother. NP
A television	costs VG	10,000 rupees. NP
This colour	suits VG	you. NP

(e) Behave-type

In this case, the verbal group takes reflexive pronouns as complements.

EXAMPLES

Sheela did not behave VG	herself Comp.	at your place. Adjunct
He prides VG	himself Comp.	on his physical strength. Adjunct
This little boy	must behave VG	himself. Comp.

(f) Lie-type

In this case, the Verbal Group can take an adverbial or a preposition phrase as complement (not a noun phrase or an adjectivial phrase).

EXAMPLES

The child	lay VG	in the pram. Prep. phr.
She	lay VG	asleep. adv.

8.3 TRANSITIVE PREDICATE PHRASE PATTERNS

8.31 Pattern III: Verbal Group + Object (+ Adjunct)

EXAMPLES

(i)	He	is playing VG	cricket Obj.	these days. Adjunct
(ii)	Everybody	knows VG	her style. Obj.	
(iii)	He	looked up VG	the word Obj.	in the dictionary. Adjunct
(iv)	You Sub.	should do VG	your duty. Obj.	
(v)	She	will bite off VG	your ear Obj.	in anger. Adjunct

8.32 Pattern IV: Verbal Group + Indirect Object + Direct Object (+ Adjunct)

EXAMPLES

(i)	I am teaching VG	you Ind. obj.	grammar. Dir. obj.		
(ii)	My father	gave VG	me Ind. obj.	a pen Dir. obj.	yesterday. Adjunct
(iii)	He VG	bought Ind. obj.	her Dir. obj.	a book.	
(iv)	Ramesh	promised VG	his beloved Ind. obj.	an excellent necklace. Dir. obj.	
(v)	He	taught VG	her Ind. obj.	linguistics. Dir. obj.	

Note: When the Direct object comes before the Indirect object, the latter takes a preposition before it.

e.g. He teaches	us Ind. obj.	English. Dir. obj.
He teaches	English	*to* us. (Notice the preposition before the Indirect object here)

8.33 Pattern V: VG + Object + Complement (+ Adjunct)

Obj. complement   Sub. complement

(This complement can be an NP, an adjective phrase, an adverbial or a prepositional phrase.)

EXAMPLES

(i)	He	left VG	her Obj.	a widow. Obj. comp. (NP)	
(ii)	He	left VG	her Obj.	a broken-hearted man. Sub. comp. (NP)	
(iii)	We	found VG	her Obj.	uncontrollable. Obj. comp. (adjective)	
(iv)	They	left VG	us Obj.	in the lurch Obj. comp. (Prep. phr.)	yesterday. Adjunct

8.4 SOME AMBIGUITIES EXPLAINED

There are some sentences (albeit unusual), which can have a double meaning according to the labels one gives to their parts. Here are a few examples:

(i) They called her a taxi.

They	called VG	her Obj.	a taxi Obj. comp.

Meaning I: They nicknamed her a 'taxi'

They	called VG	her Ind. obj.	a taxi. Dir. obj.

Meaning II: They called a taxi for her.

(ii) She made him a good wife.

She	made VG	him Obj.	a good wife. Sub. comp.

Meaning I: She proved a good wife for her husband.

She	made VG	him Obj.	a good wife. Obj. comp.

Meaning II: She made her husband play the role of 'a good wife'.

(iii) The giant tore up the street.

The giant	tore up	the street.	(Pattern-III)
	VG	Obj.	

Meaning I: The giant tore up the street into pieces.

The giant	tore	up the street.	(Pattern-II)
	VG	Comp.	

Meaning II: The giant rushed up the street.

(iv) The magician made her a steam-engine.

The magician	made	her	a steam-engine.
	VG	Ind. obj.	Dir. obj.

Meaning I: The magician made a steam-engine for her.

The magician	made	her	a steam-engine.
	VG	Obj.	Obj. comp.

Meaning II: The magician changed her into a steam-engine by magic.

Note: Part of the ambiguity is also due to the lexical meaning of specific words. If we were to replace the verbs 'called', 'made' and 'rushed' in the above sentences, the ambiguity would be lost. This opens up a problem for structural grammar as it does not take semantics into account.

SUMMARY

There are five patterns of Basic Sentences:

1. Verbal Group only
2. Verbal Group + Complement
3. Verbal Group + Object
4. Verbal Group + Indirect Object + Direct Object
5. Verbal Group + Object + Complement
   (Subject complement or Object complement)

COMPREHENSION QUESTIONS

1. Write a note on basic sentence patterns in English.
2. What are transitive predicate phrase patterns in English? Give examples.
3. List the intransitive predicate phrase patterns in English. Give examples.

4. Discuss the ambiguities in the following sentences:

(i) They called her a fool.
(ii) The magician made her an iron box.
(iii) We decided on the boat.
(iv) He left her very unhappy.
(v) He left her a widow.

5. Label the following sentences and give the pattern to which each sentence belongs: The first sentence has been solved as an illustration.

(i)	They	bought	a book.	Pattern-III
		VG	Obj.	

(ii) She passed away.
(iii) John is in Chennai (Madras).
(iv) The sky got dark.
(v) The police officer gave him a tough time.
(vi) He proved the statement false.
(vii) No birds sang.
(viii) We admired her poise.
(ix) George gave him a pen.
(x) She became a heroine.
(xi) He seemed an interesting fellow.
(xii) He is silent.
(xiii) Kanwal was in his room.
(xiv) I consider it an insult.
(xv) He proved them a good king.
(xvi) The officer turned a traitor.
(xvii) The king lay dead.
(xviii) She betrayed a bad temper.
(xix) They went to the store.
(xx) Some like it hot.

CHAPTER 9

Structuralist View of Grammar and IC Analysis

9.1 BACKGROUND TO STRUCTURAL GRAMMAR

The beginning of the twentieth century was marked by a new approach to grammar suggested by linguists like Ferdinand de Saussure and American linguists such as Franz Boas, Edward Sapir and Leonard. This school of linguistics is called **structuralism**. It arose as a reaction against the approach of the traditional grammarians of the 17th, 18th and 19th centuries.

9.11 Traditional Grammar

The traditional grammarians had looked upon Latin as their model. Since English is a member of the Indo-European family of languages, to which Latin and Greek also belong, it did have many grammatical elements in common with them. But many of these had been obscured or wholly lost as a result of extensive changes that had taken place in English. Early grammarians considered these changes as a sort of degeneration in language and felt that they were duty bound to resist these changes. They, therefore, came out with a group of prescriptive rules for English on the basis of Latin. They ignored the fact that every language is unique in its own way and has to be described as autonomous in itself. They did not realise that the only standard which is to be applied to a language is the language itself, its usage. Also, they attached more importance to the written part of language than to the spoken element. Even the definitions of the parts of speech given by them, as has been discussed earlier, were inadequate and confusing. Instead of describing the **actually spoken** language, they found faults with it on trivial considerations. The following sentences, though in common use, were condemned by them for reasons shown in brackets:

1. I do not know nothing. (double negative)
2. I will ask you to quickly do it.
   (use of 'will' with I and use of split infinitive)
3. He is taller than me.
   (comparison is between he and I and not me)

The real authority, in judgement concerning the correctness of sentences in a language, is the native speaker who uses the language, not the grammarian. The approach of the traditional grammarians was thus not scientific or logical; it was rather an illogical presumptive approach, **prescribing** certain rules of do's and don'ts as to how people should speak or write in conformity with the standards they held dear. They did not first observe as to how people used the language and then **describe** it, depending upon the usage.

The traditional grammarians gave a classicist's model of grammar based on the authority of masters of classical literature and rhetoric, while later on, after this authority was challenged (a process which began from the Renaissance onwards), models of grammar began to be made on the basis of scientific observation and analysis, i.e. the empirical approach or model was adopted.

9.12 Structural Grammar (Major Tenets)

The structural linguists began to study language in terms of observable and verifiable data and describe it according to the behaviour of the language as it was being used. These descriptive linguists emphasized the following points:

(i) *Spoken language is primary and writing is secondary.* Writing is only a means of representing speech in another medium. Speech comes earlier than writing in the life of an individual or in the development of a language.

(ii) *The synchronic study of language should take precedence over its diachronic study.* Historical considerations are not relevant to the investigation of a particular temporal state of a language. In the game of chess, for example, the situation on the board is constantly changing. But at any one time, the state of the game can be fully described in terms of the positions occupied by several pieces on the board. It does not matter by what route the players have arrived at the particular state of the game.

(iii) *Language is a system of systems.* It has a structure of its own. Each language is regarded by the structuralists as a system of relations. The elements of this system (sounds, words, etc.) have no validity independently of the relations of equivalence and contrast which hold between them. Each sound is normally meaningless in isolation. It becomes meaningful only when it combines with other sounds join to form meaningful words which further join to form sentences, i.e. units of higher level.

The structural linguists attempted to describe language in terms of its structure, as it is used, and tried to look for 'regularities' and 'patterns' or 'rules' in language structure. Bloomfield envisaged that language structure was associated with phoneme as the unit of phonology and morpheme as the unit of grammar. Phonemes are the minimal distinctive sound units of language. The word **tap**, for example, consists of three phonemes: /t/, /æ/, and /p/. Morphemes are larger than phonemes as they consist of one or more phonemes. The word **playing** consists of two morphemes **play** and **ing**, whereas it consists of the phonemes /p/, /l/, /eɪ/, /ɪ/ and /ŋ/. So in order to study the structure of a sentence, a linguist must be aware of the string of phonemes or morphemes that make up the sentence. Here is a sentence:

The unlucky player played himself out.
As a string of phonemes, it is:

/ðɪ ʌnlʌkɪ pleɪə pleɪd hɪmself aʊt/

As a string of morphemes, the structure is:

The-un-luck-y-play-er-play-ed - him-self - out.

This type of approach in respect of the structure of language was based on a desire to be completely precise, empirical, logical and scientific as against the unscientific, illogical and prescriptive approach of the traditional grammarians.

9.2 IMMEDIATE CONSTITUENT (IC) ANALYSIS

In order to study the structure of a sentence, the structural linguists thought of dividing a sentence into its immediate constituents (or ICs). The principle involved was that of cutting a sentence into two, further cutting these two parts into another two, and continuing the segmentation till the smallest unit, the morpheme was arrived at. This can be shown by taking a simple example of a sentence like:

A young girl with an umbrella chased the boy.

This sentence is made up of some natural groups. From one's intuitive knowledge of the language, the only way one may divide it into two groups is as follows:

A young girl with an umbrella	**chased the boy.**
1	2

The two parts of the sentence as shown above are called **constituents** of the sentence.

Now 1 and 2 can be further divided into natural groups as follows:

A young girl	**with an umbrella**	**chased**	**the boy.**
1-A	1-B	2-A	2-B

1-A and 1-B are the **constituents** of 1 while 2-A and 2-B are the constituents of 2.

The above information can be displayed in the form of a **tree diagram** as follows:

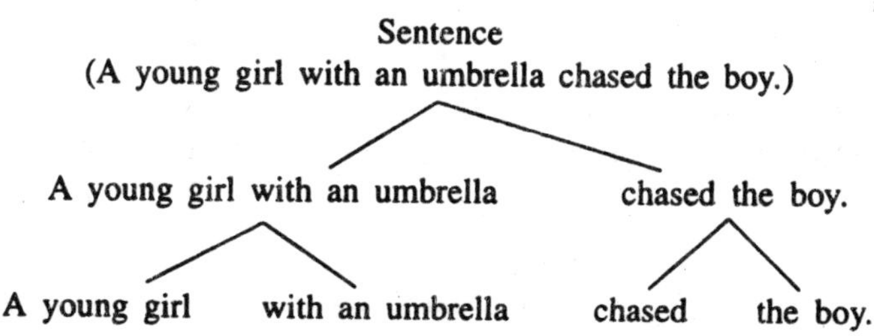

Now, 1-A, 1-B, 2-A, and 2-B can be further subdivided into smaller constituents as follows:

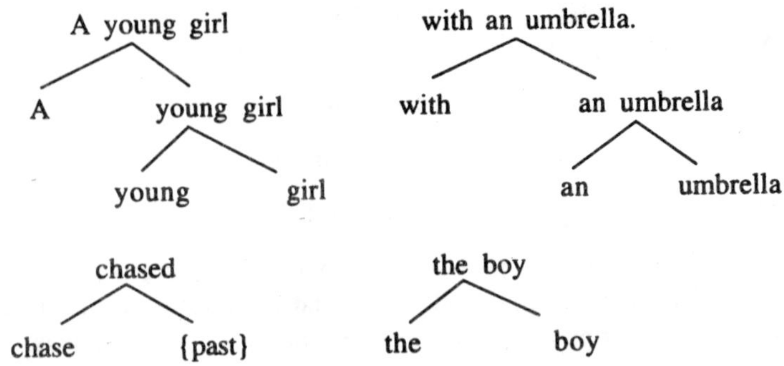

This type of analysis of a sentence is called **Immediate Constituent Analysis.** Every constituent is a part of a higher natural word group and every constituent is further divided into lower constituents. This process goes on till one arrives at the smallest constituent, a morpheme that can no longer be further divided. The full IC analysis of the above sentence is given below:

A young girl with an umbrella chased the boy

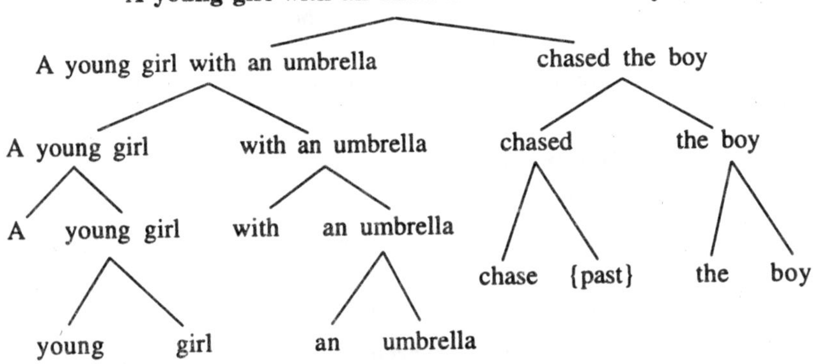

These constituents can also be labelled as belonging to different grammatical constituents like Noun phrase, Verb phrase, Adverbial, and Prep. phrase, which can be further divided into categories such as Noun, Adjective, Verb, and Tense Morpheme. Different methods are used for showing the immediate constituents. Some of these are given below:

(a) Segmentation using vertical lines

A | | young | | | girl | | with | | | an | | | | umbrella | chase | | | d | | the | | | boy

(b) Segmentation using brackets

[[[(A)] [(young)(girl)]] [[with] [(an)(umbrella)]]] [[(chase) (d)] [(the) (boy)]]]

(c) Segmentation using a tree diagram

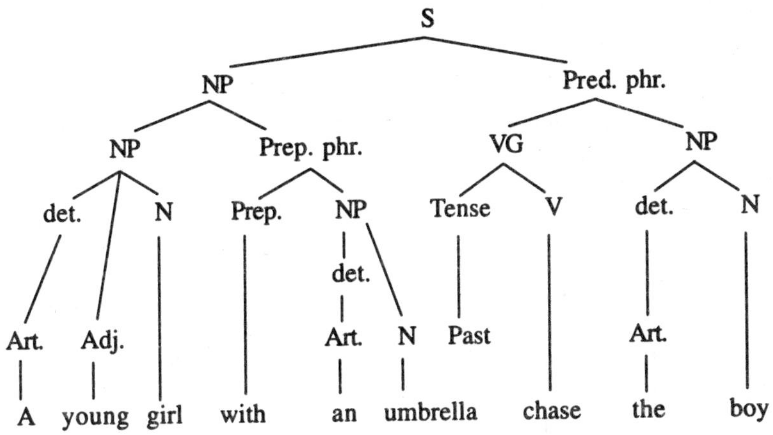

Now, the question arises as to how we should make the cuts. The answer lies in the notion of 'expansion'. A sequence of morphemes that patterns like another sequence is said to be an expansion of it. One sequence can, in such cases, be replaced by another as similar sequence patterns will appear in the same kind of environment. Here is an example of similar sequences in expansion that can fit into the same slot:

1. Daffodils
2. Yellow daffodils
3. The yellow daffodils
4. The yellow daffodils with a lovely look.

The elements 1, 3, 4 are expansions in the above set, i.e. "daffodils" is the **head** word, whereas the other words in 2, 3, and 4 are modifiers. Incidentally, the set of examples given above can be grouped under the term **Noun Phrase (NP).**

A noun phrase may be a single word, a single noun or pronoun, or a group of words that belong with the noun and cluster around it. A noun phrase has in it a noun (a Head word) and certain **modifiers**. Generally, a noun in a noun phrase (optionally) has the following modifiers appearing before it in the given order:

1. Restrictor : Words like: especially, only, merely, just, almost, particularly, even
2. Pre-determiners : Words like: half, double, both, one-third, twice, all of
3. Determiners : These words include
   (a) Articles: a/an, the
   (b) Demonstratives: this, that, these, those
   (c) Possessives: my, his, own, Ram's
4. Ordinals : Words like: first, third, last, next
5. Quantifiers : Words like: many, several, few, less
6. Adjective phrase : good, long, tall, or intensifier and adjective, e.g. very good, or adjective and adjective, e.g. good, nice looking

7. Classifier : a **city** college
a **leather** purse
a **summer** dress

Here are some examples of noun phrases (shown in the form of tree diagrams) referred to above.

His last play

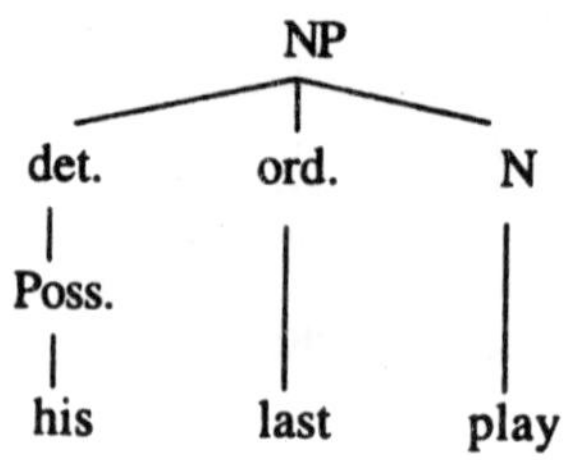

A very nice shirt

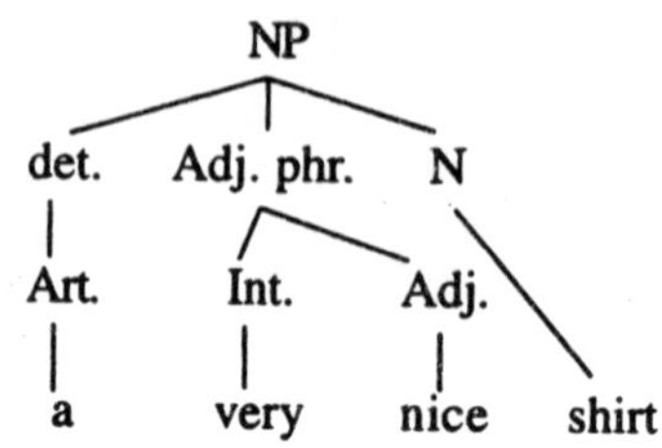

All the famous victories

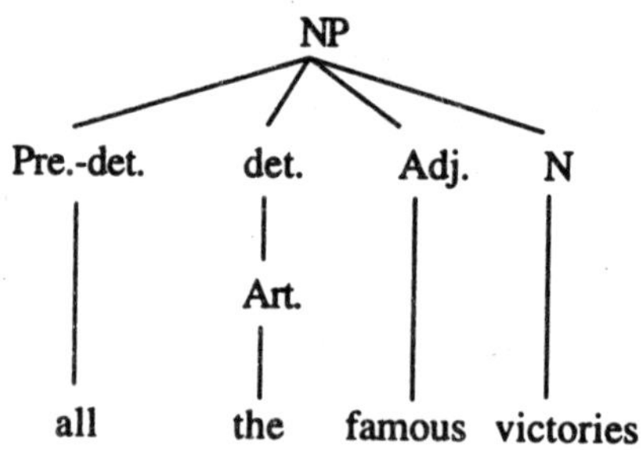

Her old leather shoes

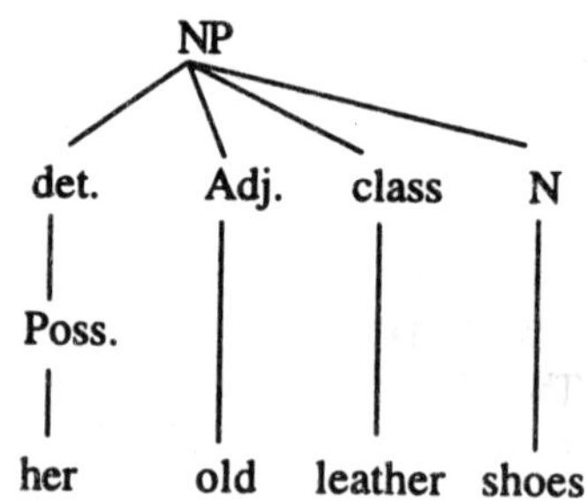

Here are some other examples of NP:

Boys and girls

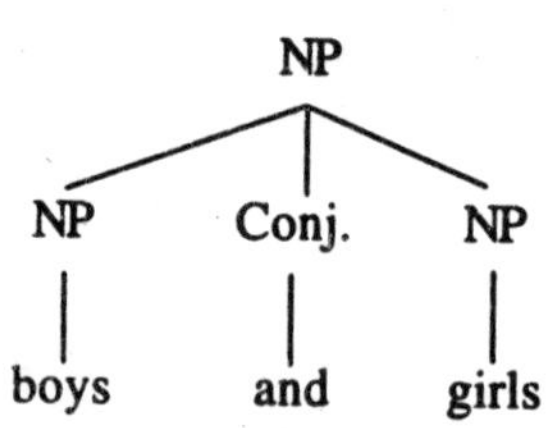

The man who fired a shot

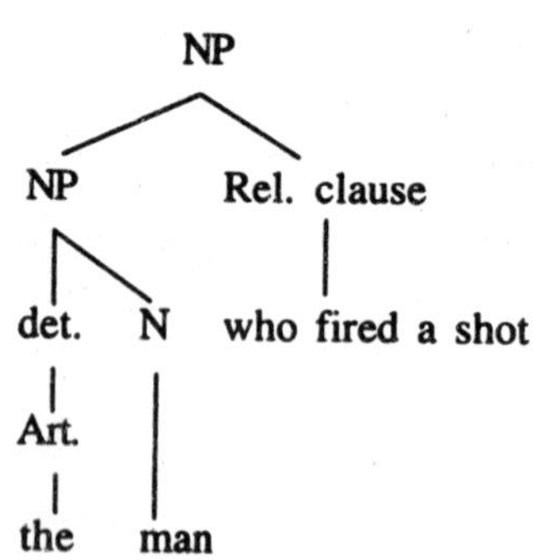

Preposition phrase

A Prepositional phrase is a Noun phrase preceded by a preposition, i.e.

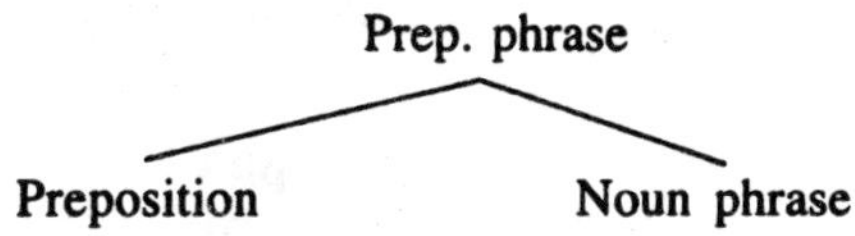

Here is an example: **On the table**

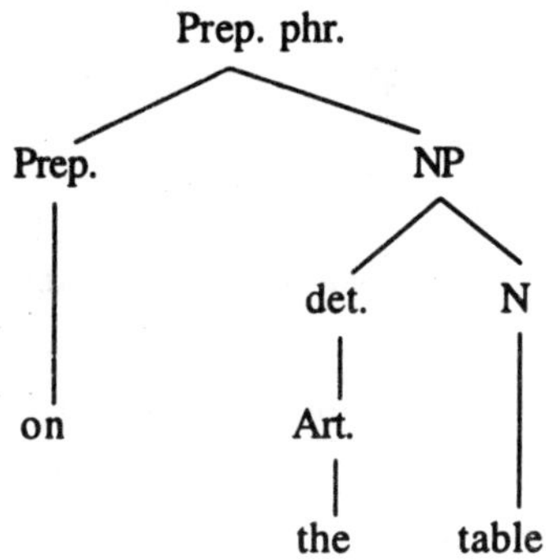

Sometimes, a Noun phrase contains a Preposition phrase embedded in it. In such cases, the Noun phrase can be broken up into NP and preposition phrase. Both can then be further split up. Here is an example:

The boy on the bridge

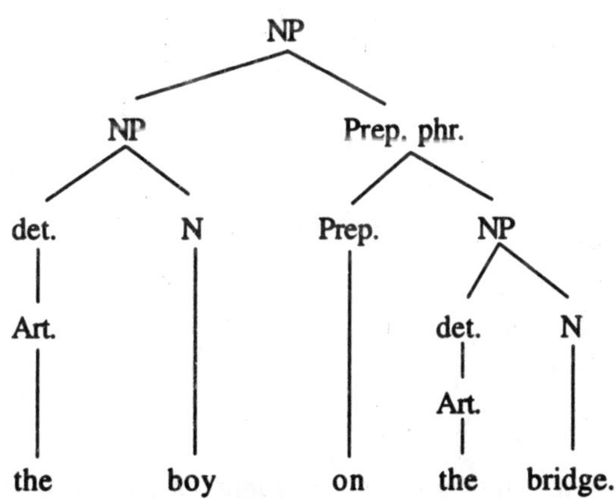

The Verbal Group (VG). The Verbal group generally immediately follows the NP in a typical English sentence, e.g.

Ram	**plays**
NP	VG
Ram	**is playing**
NP	VG

Ram	**has been playing**
NP	VG
Ram	**can play**
NP	VG

The main (or basic) verb in all these sentences is **play**. The Verbal group consists of the main verb and the auxiliary.

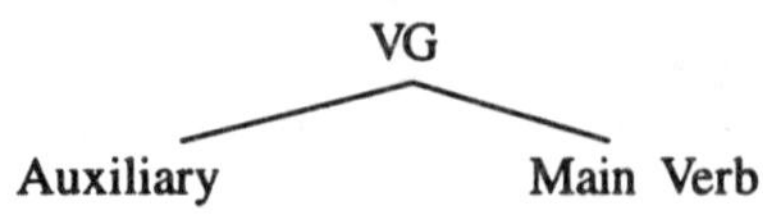

Auxiliary, in turn, is made up of the **tense** (compulsory item) and any **one or more** of the following items:

- **Modal** (marked by modal auxiliaries like can, may, will, shall, must).
- **Perfective** (marked by **have + en**, where **en** is a marker of the past participle morpheme)
- **Progressive** (marked by **be + ing**)

The whole information can be presented in the form of a tree diagram:

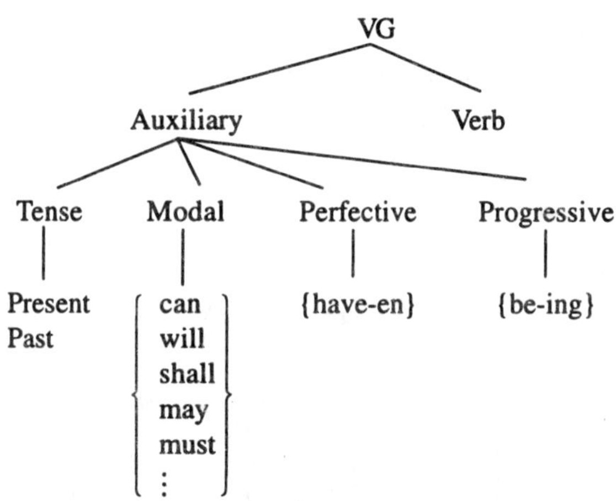

It should be noted that modern linguists admit of only **two** tenses in English: Present and Past. English can express present time, past time and future time, but it does not mean that it has three tenses too. Look at the following sentences:

He is playing a match now.
(Present tense, Present time)

He is playing a match next Sunday.
(Present tense, Future time)

If I went to Bombay, I would bring a camera for you.
(Past tense, Future time)

Tense, it **may** be stated here, is a grammatical category seen in the **form** or **shape** of the verb. Normally, in English, tense is realized as

–e(s) (present)
–e(d) (past)

In the expressions **will play** or **will eat, will** is in the present tense, the past form of which is **would.**

In a classical language like Sanskrit which has **three** tenses, these are shown in the three different **forms** the basic verb takes, while referring to the present, past or future time, **e.g.**

basic verb: [pʌʈɦ]	[pʌʈɦ ṭi:]	(present tense form)	:	reads
	[pʌʈɦ ṭəɦ]	(past tense form)	:	read
	[pʌʈɦ ɪʃjəṭi:]	(future tense form)	:	will read

Corresponding to this, there are only two such forms in English, e.g. plays, play**ed.**

The use of modals **shall/will** is only **one** of the mechanisms of expressing the **future time**. Also, will/shall do not **always** express the future time, e.g.

Sita will be at home now (Present time).

Also, it should be noted that while tense and the main verb are the compulsory segments of a verbal group, the modal, the perfective and the progressive are only optional items. Given below are some model analyses of some verbal groups:

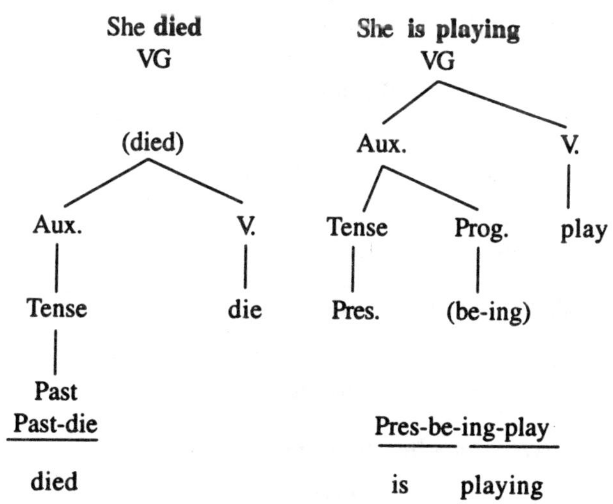

He **had been writing**

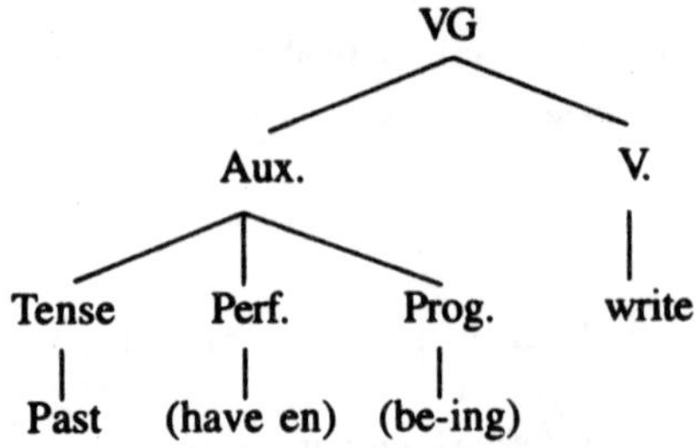

Past - have- en - be-ing - write

had been writing

I **have finished**

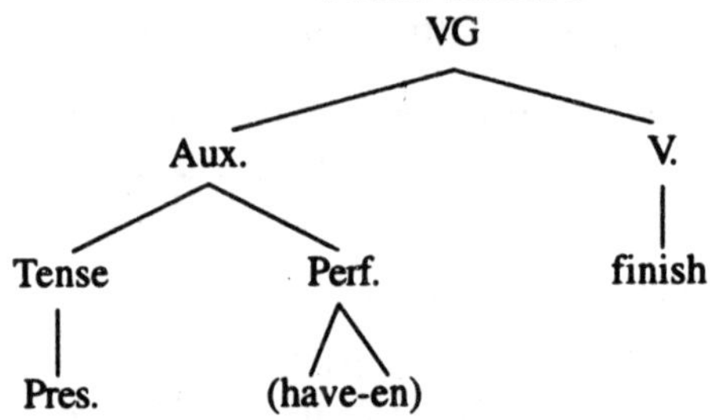

Pres- have- en - finish

have finished

She **might have been crying**

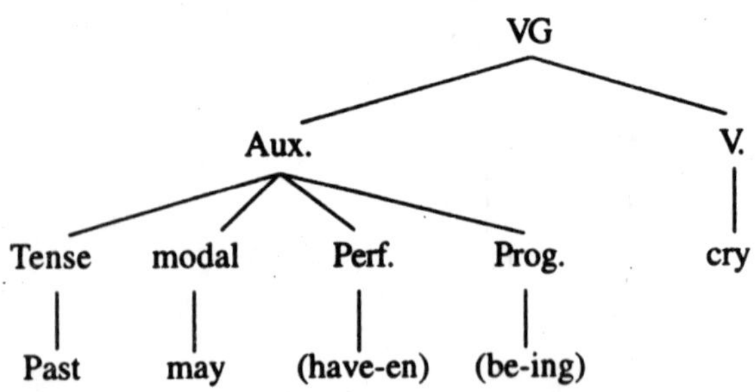

Past - may - have - **en - be -ing - cry**

might been crying

Adverbials

Any group of words that performs the function of an **adverb** is called an *adverbial.* It may consist of a single word, a phrase or a clause. It generally specifies **time,**

place, **manner**, **reason**, etc., and modifies a verb, an adjective or a fellow adverb. Given below are some sentences in which the adverbials are put in italics:

She slept *soundly.*
He spoke *fluently.*
We have approached him *a number of times.*
He smokes *heavily.*
He spoke *in a nice manner.*
I shall see you *in a day or so.*
I went there *as fast as I could.*
She left home *when she was a young girl.*
Where there is a will there is a way.
He talks *as if she were a fool.*

9.3 IC ANALYSIS OF SENTENCES*

A single sentence is made up of an NP (subject) and a predicate phrase. This predicate phrase, apart from a compulsory verbal group, may optionally have one or more noun phrase(s), preposition phrase(s), adverbials and adjective phrases. Here are a few examples:

(i) Rahul Dravid has been playing cricket for many years.

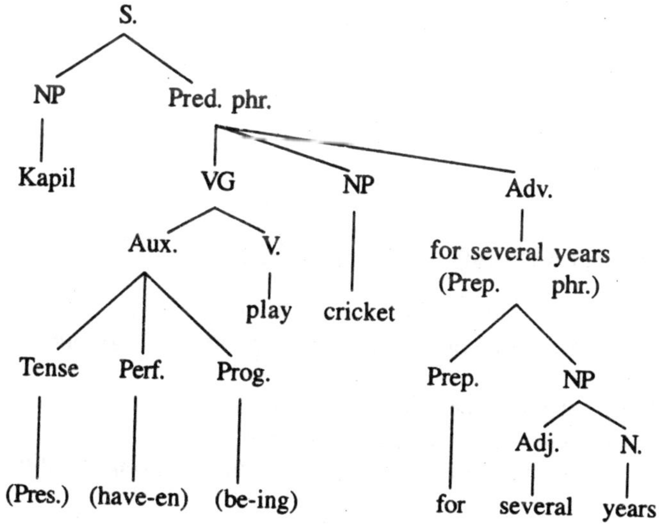

* Keeping in view the scope of the present book, only **simple** sentences have been dealt with here.

(ii) After depositing the fee the boys went to the hostel.

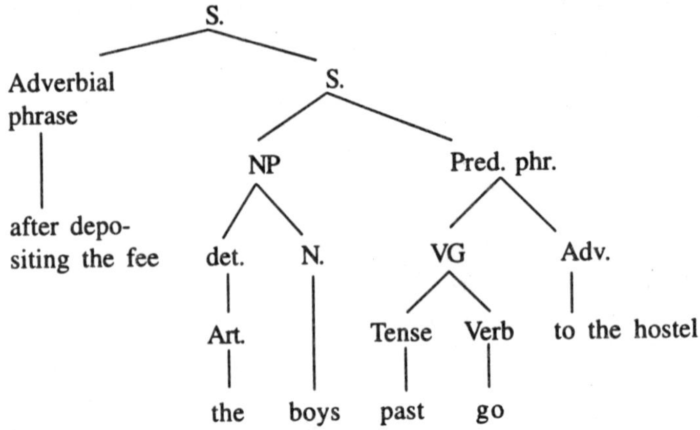

(iii) These girls have been singing nicely.

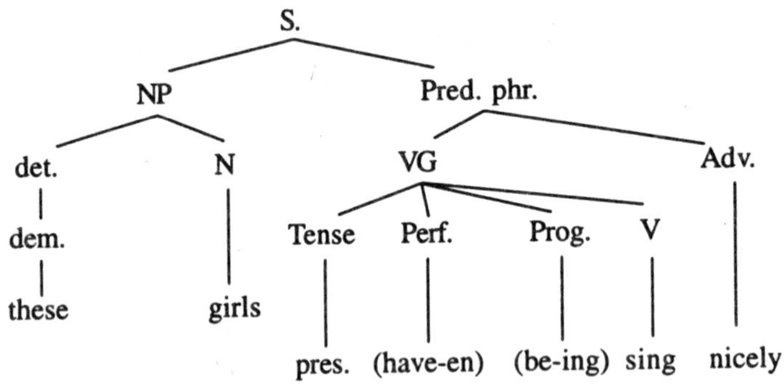

9.4 LIMITATIONS OF IC ANALYSIS

Immediate constituent analysis has its limitations. It is not possible to analyse such structures, as they do not form proper grammatical groups. For example, here is a sentence:

She is taller than her sister.

In this sentence, the sequence **-er than** is not covered by IC analysis. Such a sequence can be explained in terms of the following constituents only:

- She is tall.
- She has a sister.
- The sister is short.

Similarly, there are several cases of sentences that are ambiguous, e.g. Time flies. It can have two meanings:

- Time is flying.
- Time the flies (*Time* as verb).

(iv) **The girl with a white dress | has been singing | lovely songs | since morning**

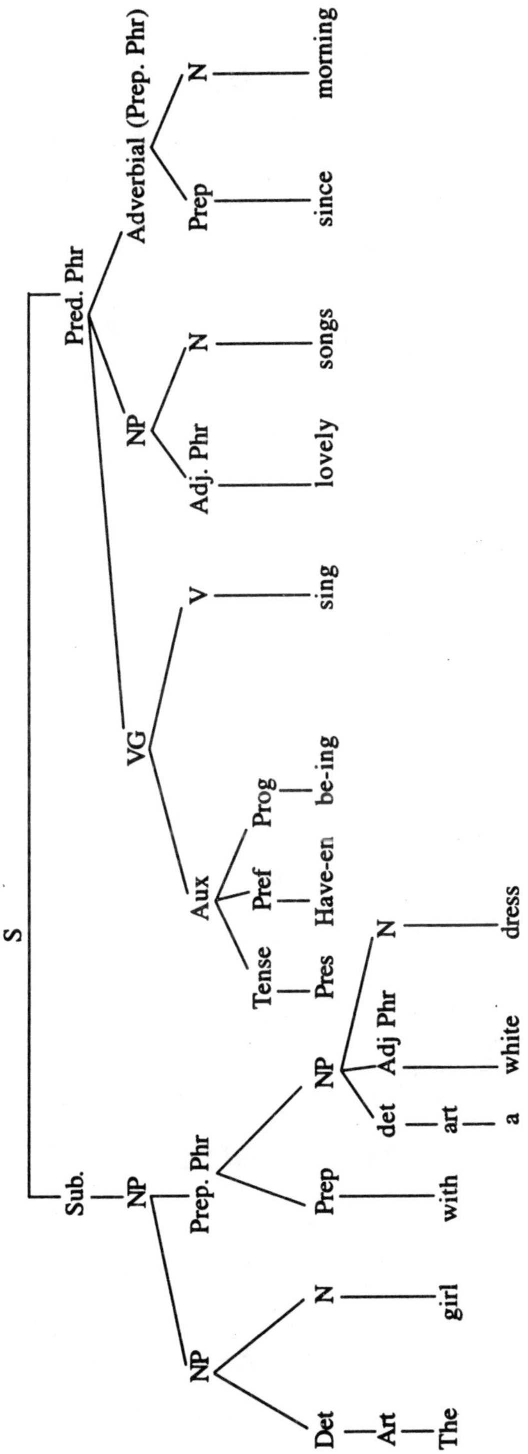

(v) Boys and girls | may join | the group | in the evening

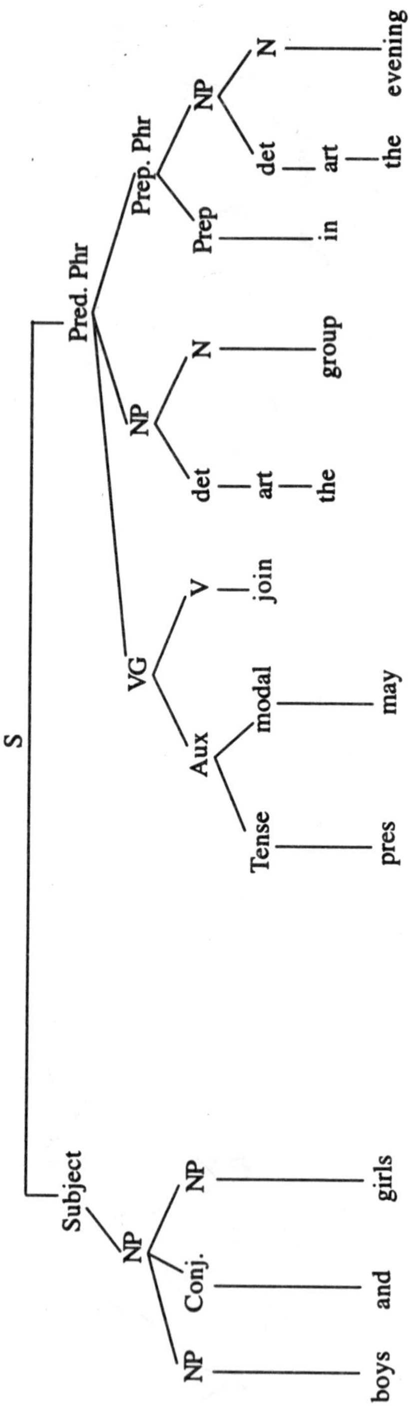

In such a case, only proper labelling can solve the problem. There are, however, some sentences that are structurally similar but semantically they are different. An oft-quoted example is:

- John is easy to flatter.
- John is eager to flatter.

Such sentences cannot be explained by IC analysis unless they are broken up into simple pairs of sentences. In the case of the two sentences above, we may have the following groups:

- (It) is easy. Someone flatters John.
- John is eager. He wants to flatter.

Many a time, overlapping ICs also cause a problem. For example, here is a sentence:

He has no interest in, or taste for, music.
This sentence means to convey:
He has **no** interest in music.
He has **no** taste for music.

The word **no** applies to both **interest** and **taste.** It is not possible to show this in IC analysis.

Also, IC analysis fails to show such elements as remain unstated in a sentence, e.g. in the sentence:

Hit the ball

who is being addressed? The element '**you**' is missing here. There is no way of showing this in IC analysis. Not only that. IC analysis fails to show relationship between sentence types such as active and passive, affirmative and negatives, statements and questions. Look at the following sets of sentences which, though semantically similar, have different structures:

(i) Who does not love his motherland?
Everybody loves his motherland.
(ii) Kapil hit a six.
A six was hit by Kapil.
(iii) Everybody in the hall wept.
There was none in the hall but wept.

Grammarians realise the limitations of IC analysis and have to take to other means also (e.g. TG grammar) to fully explain the structure of sentences.

9.5 PHRASE STRUCTURE RULES (PS RULES)

The structure of phrases, as discussed above, can be summed up in the following notation that gives the structure of the concerned phrase in a straight line. Here is a summary of the PS-Rules.

S ⟶ NP + Pred. phr.

NP ⟶ Restrictor - Pre-determiner-determiner-Ordinal-
Quantifier - Adjective phrase - Classifier-noun

Pred. phr. ⟶ VG – | NP / Prep. phr. / Adj. phr. / Adverbial |

VG ⟶ Aux. + V

Aux. ⟶ Tense + (Modal) + (Perfective) + (Progressive)

Prep. phr. ⟶ Prep + NP

NP ⟶ NP + Prep. phr.

SUMMARY

As a reaction to the traditional approach to language study, there arose in the 20th century a group of linguists called **Structuralists**. Representative figures in this group were Franz Boas, Edward Sapir and Bloomfield. The structuralists felt that linguistics has to be **descriptive** rather than **prescriptive**. Any study of a language, they said, should be based on the observable and verifiable **facts** of the language. They emphasized the following points:

1. Speech is primary; writing is only secondary.
2. The synchronic study of language is more important than the diachronic study.
3. Language is a system of systems. It has a structure of its own.

The structural linguists tried to describe language in terms of its structures as it was being used. They tried to look for 'patterns' or 'regularities' in language structures. They envisaged that language structure was associated with **phoneme** as the unit of phonology and **morpheme** as the unit of grammar. This approach was desired to be completely precise, empirical, logical and scientific.

In order to study the structure of sentences, the structural linguists thought of dividing a sentence into its **immediate constituents**. This process is known as IC analysis. Different methods (segmentation, bracketing, tree diagrams) were used for showing the immediate constituents.

A sentence is said to consist of an NP and a Predicate phrase. The Predicate phrase consists of a Verbal group and one or more Noun phrase(s), Adjective phrase(s), Adverbials and Preposition phrases.

Here is an example:

Kapil **has been playing cricket for many years.**
NP Pred. phr.

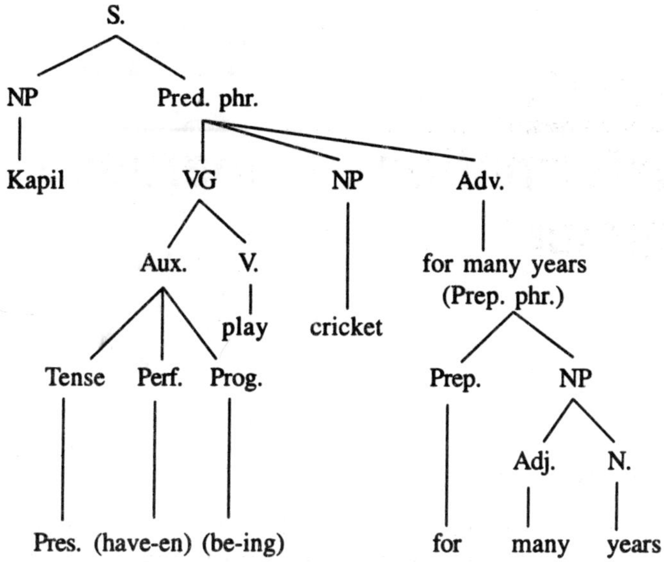

A summary of PS rules governing the IC analysis has already been given above.

COMPREHENSION QUESTIONS

1. What are the main tenets of structuralism? Explain.
2. What is a Noun phrase? What are its important constituents?
3. Write a note on:
   (a) Preposition phrase
   (b) Verbal group
   (c) Adverbials
4. Give an IC analysis of the following sentences:
   (a) He has already resigned.
   (b) I have been cursing my luck for several years.
   (c) He can tell a lie.
   (d) I plan to go there after the rains.
   (e) He appeared in the court.
5. Write a note on IC analysis. What are its limitations?

CHAPTER 10

Transformational Generative Grammar

10.1 INTRODUCTION

Transformational Generative grammar (TG) had its first exponent in Noam Chomsky, an American linguist. In his book *Syntactic Structures* (1957), and later in *Aspects of the Theory of Syntax* (1965), Chomsky tried to answer several questions left unanswered by the structuralists. Structuralism, as has been discussed earlier, is primarily **corpus** bound, that is, it analyses the data of a given corpus by **inductive** methods. Chomsky, on the other hand, takes a **deductive** approach, in building a theoretical account of grammar. His grammar attempts to explain how the competence of a native speaker of a language can enable that speaker to produce an infinite number of sentences from a finite set. Not only are the sentences generated **grammatical,** but they are also **meaningful.** While structuralism took into account the form (phoneme and morpheme are units of form rather than meaning), TG grammar considers the relation between form and meaning as crucial in the generation of sentences that are both grammatical and meaningful. Chomsky gives the example of the sentence 'Colorless green ideas sleep furiously' to show that a sentence can be grammatically correct and yet not make sense, therefore the grammar does not generate sentences like these. Structural grammar also fails to account for ambiguities in sentences, since these occur at the level of meaning.

10.2 DEEP AND SURFACE STRUCTURE

An adequate grammar must provide for the facts of the language that it is **productive, complex** and **arbitrary**. It must establish the relationship of various sentences and account for the **deep** and **surface** structure of sentences. It must, for example, explain the relationship between sets of sentences like:

1. (a) He wrote a letter.
   (b) A letter was written by him.
2. (a) Why did you go there?
   (b) You went there for some reason.
3. (a) Where do you live?
   (b) You live somewhere.

As the name implies, TG grammar is both **transformational** and **generative.** It goes a step further from the structural grammar. It not only analyses the sentences, divides them into parts and shows the functions of various parts but also completely rearranges them and shows the inter-relatedness between sentences. It takes up the **basic** or **kernel** sentence first. A basic or a kernel sentence, it may be pointed out, **is simple, assertive, declarative,** and **active** in form. Here are some examples:

Kernel sentences

John is playing football.
I wrote a letter.
You spoke the truth.

Non-kernel sentences

Is John playing football? (Interrogative)
John is not playing football. (Negative)
A letter was written by me. (Passive)
Who wrote the letter? (Question form)
Why did you speak the truth? (Question form)
You spoke the truth when you were forced. (Complex sentence)
You did not speak the truth. (Negative)
You spoke the truth but told a new story. (Compound sentence)

All the non-kernel structures or complicated structures can be thought of as having been derived from their kernel forms with the help of some **transformations.** A sentence like: **Where did you go yesterday?** can be derived from the kernel sentence: **You went somewhere yesterday** by applying certain **transformations.**

Transformational analysis not only shows the inter-relatedness between sentences but also explains the ambiguities between sentences that appear identical but are **transforms** from different kernels. Here is, for example, a sentence:

Flying planes can be dangerous.

The sentence is ambiguous for we cannot tell what is dangerous, the planes that fly or the act of flying planes. We can, however, resolve this ambiguity by showing that the same sentence can be analysed as being transforms from two different sets of kernel sentences. The present sentence can be derived from the following two different sets:

(a) Some people fly planes. This can be dangerous.
(b) Planes fly. They can be dangerous.

Similarly, here is another set of sentences:

(a) I expected Kapil to hit a six.
(b) I asked Kapil to hit a six.

The two sentences have the same surface structure but their deep structures are different. These deep structures are:

(a) (i) I expected (something).
(ii) Kapil hits a six.

(b) (i) I asked Kapil (something).
(ii) He hits a six.

Another pair of sentences that can be quoted in this context is:

(a) Raja is eager to please.
(b) Raja is easy to please.

The Kernel sentences for (a) are:

(i) Raja is eager (for something).
(ii) He pleases (someone).

The Kernel sentences for (b), however, are:

(i) It is easy.
(ii) Someone pleases Raja.

Examples can be multiplied but what needs to be noted here is that while a set of two sentences may have the same surface structure, they may have different deep structures. It is through TG grammar alone that one can apply different transformations to the kernel sentences to arrive at the desired surface structures.

It must by now be apparent that a kernel sentence has to be first analysed with the help of Phrase structure rules as discussed under Immediate Constituent Analysis and then made to pass through transformational rules to arrive at a surface structure. A kernel sentence is the **deep** structure to which a string of transformations is applied to **generate** the surface structure. TG grammar is revolutionary in the sense that it presents a system that gives us an idea of the possible process in which a child learns a language or produces an infinite variety of sentences many of which he or she has not heard earlier. Thus TG grammar illustrates how we get from one state, or stage, in a language to another. It does not merely describe a given sentence, it does much more as it provides descriptions of a great many of the possible sentences in the language. A native speaker of a language understands both, the deep structure as well as the surface structure of a sentence. He can easily apply the various transformational rules to produce sentences which he has never heard before. That is what Chomsky meant when he talked of the **competence** (the intuitive knowledge of a speaker of a language about the system of his language) and **performance** (the actual production of language) of a user of a language.

It would be useful to list the various PS rules that have been spelt out in the previous chapters:

1. S → NP + Pred. phr.	(S ——— Sentence) (NP —— Noun phrase)

2. NP → Res.-Predet.-det.-Ord.-quant.-Adj. phr.-class-N

3. Pred. phr. → VG +	NP Prep. phr. Adj. phr. Adj.	NP Prep. phr. Adj. phr. Adj.	+ ——

4. VG → Aux.-V

5. Aux. → Tense-{Modal}-{Perf.}-{Prog.}-{Pass.}

6. Tense → | Present / Past |

7. Modal → | Will / Shall / Can / May |

8. Perf. → have-en

9. Prog. → be-ing

10. Pass. → be-en

11. Prep. phr. → Prep.-NP

10.3 TRANSFORMATIONAL RULES

Rule I: ***Interrogative rule***

NP-tense	be have modal	**Interrogative tense** ⟶	be have modal	-NP

Rule II: ***Affix switch rule***

-Tense	Modal main verb	⟶	Modal main verb	-Tense
-ing	have be		have be	-ing
-en	do		do	-en

Here are some **examples** involving the application of these rules for deriving the surface structure of sentences from their kernels:

1. **Surface structures:** Is he sleeping?
   The kernel sentence or the deep structure in the case of this sentence is: He is sleeping.
   Analysis : He - pres. - be - ing - sleep.
   Interr. : pres - be - he - ing - sleep.
   Affix : **be - pres.** - he - **sleep - ing**
   (is) (sleeping)

2. Has Ram been playing a match? (Surface Structure)
   Ram has been playing a match (Kernel).
   Analysis : Ram - pres. - have - en - be - ing - play - a match.
   Interr. : Pres. - have - Ram - en - be - ing - play-a match.
   Affix : **have - pres.** - Ram - **be - en - play-ing** a match.
   (has) (been) (playing)

3. Could you repeat the trick?
   Kernel sentence : You could repeat the trick.

Analysis : You - past - can - repeat - the trick.
Interr. : **past - can** - you - repeat - the trick.
Affix : **Can - past** - you - repeat - the trick.
(could)

4. Have you seen the Taj?
Kernel sentence : You have seen the Taj.
Analysis : You - pres - have - en - see - the Taj.
Interr. : Pres - have - you - en - see - the Taj.
Affix : **Have - pres.** - you - **see - en** - the Taj.
(have) (seen)

5. Would he join the party?
Kernel sentence : He would join the party.
Analysis : He - past - will - join - the party.
Interr. : **Past - will -** he - join - the party.
Affix : **Will - past - he -** join - the party.
(would)

Rule III: ***Do-support rule.*** In some sentences, a **do-support** has to be supplied. Here is an example:

Surface structure : Did John see her?
Kernel sentence : John saw her.
Analysis : John-past-see-her.
Interr. : past-John-see-her.

Here is a situation where, as a result of the **interrogative rule**, only the **tense** is placed outside the **NP** as there is no **be** or **have** or **modal** attached to the **tense.** Now, the **tense** is a **Bound Morpheme.** It cannot stand alone. It must be attached to some verbal element (not to any **NP** like **John**). Therefore, a dummy verb, namely **do,** is supplied here to be attached to the **tense.** This rule is called **do-support** rule. It says: Support the **tense** with **do** when **tense** is followed by a non-verbal item. So the third step in the above series of transformations is:

Do-support: past - **do** - John - see - him.
Now, one can apply the affix-switch rule.
Affix: do-past - John - see - him.
(did)

EXAMPLE Derive the structure: Did Sita accept your proposal?

Kernel : Sita accepted your proposal.
Analysis : Sita - past - accept - your - proposal.
Interr. : **Past** - Sita - accept - your - proposal.
Do-support : past - **do -** Sita - accept - your - proposal.
Affix : **do - past** - Sita - accept - your - proposal.
(did)

Wh-type question

In order to derive wh-type questions, two more transformation rules have to be applied. These rules are:

(i) wh-substitution
(ii) wh-fronting

The following examples will make it clear as to how, and in what order, these rules are applied.

Surface structure: Why did you punish him?

Kernel	:	You punished him **for some reason.**
Analysis	:	You - past - punish - him - for some reason.
Wh-subs.	:	You - past - punish - him - **why.**
Interr.	:	**past** - you - punish - him - why.
Wh-front	:	**Why** - past - you - punish - him.
Do-supp.	:	Why - past - **do** - you - punish - him.
Affix	:	Why - **do-past** - you - punish - him. (did)

It may be noted that the order in which the T-Rules are applied is:

(i) W — Wh substitution
(ii) I — Interrogative rule
(iii) W — Wh-fronting
(iv) D — Do-support
(v) A — Affix-switch rule

A kernel sentence may need **some** or **all** of these transformations to arrive at the surface structure. The order of transformation rules, however, remains the same in all cases.

MORE EXAMPLES:

1. Where did you stay last night?

Kernel: You stayed **somewhere** last night.

Analysis	:	You - past - stay - somewhere - last night.
Wh-sub.	:	You - past - stay - **where** - last night.
Interr.	:	**past** - you - stay - where - last night.
Wh-front	:	**Where** - past - you - stay - last night.
Do-supp.	:	Where - past - **do** - you - stay - last night.
Affix	:	Where - **do - past** - you - stay - last night. (did)

2. How did you learn all this?

Kernel: You learnt all this **somehow.**

Analysis	:	You - past - learn - all this - somehow.
Wh-sub.	:	You - past - learn - all this - **how.**

Wh-front : **How** - past - you - learn - all this.
Do-supp : How - past - **do**- you - learn - all this.
Affix : How - **do - past** - you - learn - all this.
(did)

3. When has he returned from UK?

Kernel: He has returned from UK **at some time.**
Analysis : He - pres. - have - en - return - from UK - at some time.
Wh-sub. : He - pres. - have - en - return - from UK - **When.**
Interr. : **pres. - have** - he - en - return - from UK.
Wh-front : **When** - pres. - have - he - en - return - from UK.
Affix : When - **have - pres.** - he - **return - en** - from UK.
(has) (returned)

(*Note*: It may be noted that this derivation **does not** need a Do-support rule).

4. What does Linguistics teach you?

Kernel: Linguistics teaches you **something.**
Analysis : Linguistics - pres. - teach - you - something.
Wh-sub. : Linguistics - pres. - teach - you - **what**.
Interr. : **pres.** - Linguistics - teach - you - what.
Wh-front : **What** - pres. - Linguistics - teach - you.
Do-supp : What - pres. - **do** - Linguistics - teach - you.
Affix : What **- do - pres.** - Linguistics - teach - you.
(does)

5. Who presided over the meeting?

Kernel: Someone presided over the meeting.
Analysis : Someone - past - preside over - the meeting.
Wh-sub. : **Who** - past - preside - over the meeting.
Interr. : **past** - who - preside over - the meeting.
Wh-front : who - past - preside over - the meeting.
Affix : who **- preside over - past** - the meeting.
(presided over)

Negation

Negation rule is another of the important rules of transformation. This rule is applied as follows:

	Modal			Modal	
Tense-		**Neg.**	Tense-		
	be	⟶		be	-not
	have			have	

(*Note:* If there is no **modal** or **be** or **have**, after the **tense, not** is placed directly after the **tense**, i.e.

Tense **Neg.** Tense-not
⟶

EXAMPLES

1. **Surface structure:** I will not go.
   Deep structure or Kernel sentence: I will **go.**
   Analysis : I - pres. - will - go.
   Neg. : I - pres. - will - **not** - go.
   Affix : I - **will - pres.** - not - go.
   (will)

2. **Surface structure:** He did not go.
   Kernel : He went.
   Analysis : He - past - go.
   Neg. : He - past - **not** - go.
   Do-supp. : He - past **- do -** not - go.
   Affix : He - **do - past** - not - go.
   (did)

Negative contraction rule

Not $\xrightarrow{\textbf{neg. cont.}}$ **n't**

(*Note:* When **not** is contracted to n't, it is attached closely to the verbal item preceding it, i.e. to modal, be or tense, **n't** moves wherever these items move).

EXAMPLES

1. Did not he play the match?
   Kernel: He played the match.
   Analysis : He - past - play - the match.
   Neg. : He - past - not - play - the match.
   Neg.cont. : He - past - **n't** - play - the match.
   Interr. : **past n't -** he - play - the match.
   Do-supp : past **- do-** n't - he - play - the match.
   Affix : **do-past-n't** - he - play - the match.
   (did n't)

2. Is not he a fool?
   Kernel: He is a fool.
   Analysis : He - pres. - be - a fool.
   Neg. : He - pres. - be - **not** - a fool.
   Neg.cont. : He - pres. - be **n't** - a fool.
   Interr. : **Pres. - be -** n't - he - a fool.
   Affix : **Be - pres. - n't** - he - a fool.
   (Isn't)

3. Why didn't you speak the truth?
   Kernel: You spoke the truth **for some reason.**

Analysis	:	You - past - speak - the truth - for some reason.
Wh-sub.	:	You - past - speak - the truth - **why.**
Neg.	:	You - past - **not** - speak - the truth - why.
Neg.cont.	:	You - past - **n't** - speak - the truth - why.
Interr.	:	**past - n't -** you - speak - the truth - why.
Wh-front	:	**Why** - past - n't - you - speak - the truth.
Do-supp.	:	Why - past **- do -** n't - you - speak - the truth.
Affix	:	Why **-do-past-not-** you - speak - the truth. (didn't)

Passivisation

(i) Passivisation rule

$$NP_1 - Aux. - V - NP_2 \xrightarrow{\textbf{Pass.}} NP_2 - Aux. - \textbf{be - en} - V - by - NP_1$$

(*Note:* If the subject of the active sentence is **one** or **someone**, it can be deleted after passivisation by applying the **Agent deletion rule**).

EXAMPLES

1. **Surface structure:** She was seen by him.

Kernel	:	He saw her.
Analysis	:	He - past - see - her.
Pass.	:	She - past **- be - en** - see - **by** him.
Affix	:	She - **be - past - see - en** - by - him. (was) (seen)

2. Orders have been obeyed.

Kernel: (They) have obeyed the orders.

Analysis	:	They - pres. - have - en - obey - the orders.
Pass	:	The orders - pres. - have - en - be-en - obey - by them.
Affix	:	The orders - have - pres. - be - en - obey - en -by them.
Agent del	:	**The orders - have - pres. - be - en - obey - en.** (have) (been) (obeyed)

3. The match will be won by us.

Kernel: We will win the match.

Analysis	:	We - pres. - will - win - the match.
Pass	:	The match - pres. - will - be - en - win - by us.
Affix	:	The match - **will-pres.** - be - **win-en-** by us. (will) (won)

We have so far discussed (within the scope of this introductory book) cases of interrogatives, negatives and passives only for simple sentences. Transformational rules, as has been seen, help us to understand the operations that go on in the mind of the child as he frames complicated language structures in his mind. TG rules are generative in the sense that with the help of TG rules one can produce any number of **possible** sentences in the language.

It may, however, be pointed out that the **TG grammar** has its own limitations. Research in the field of grammar is a continuing process. Many new theories, e.g. the Montaigue Grammar, Fillmore's Case Grammar, Scale and Category Grammar or Systemic Grammar based on the Firthian School, have come up. May be, in the years to come, we may have better theories of grammar that provide more insights into the learning and teaching of languages.

SUMMARY

Transformational Generative Grammar (TGG) answered several questions that the structuralists had left unanswered. Structuralism does not take cognizance of the fact of **competence** of a native speaker of the language to produce an **infinite** number of sentences. Language is **productive** and **complex**. A sentence has a **deep** structure and a **surface** structure. It is the result of several **transformations** applied to a deep structure (a kernel sentence) that one arrives at the **surface** structure of a sentence. TG grammar shows this inter-relatedness between different sentences. It also helps to remove ambiguities between sentences that appear identical but are **transforms** from different Kernels. Some of the important transformational rules are as follows: **1s1**

1. **Interrogative rule**

NP - tense	be	**Interrogative**	**tense**	be	
	have	⟶		have	-NP
	modal			modal	

2. **Affix switch rule**

-Tense	Modal		Modal	-Tense
	main		main	
	verb	**Affix**	verb	
-ing	have	⟶	have	-ing
	be		be	
-en	do		do	-en

3. **Do-support rule**

Tense- (NP) **Do-supp.** ⟶ Tense-do- (NP)

4. **Negation rule**

	Modal			Modal	
Tense-		**Neg.**	Tense-		
	be	⟶		be	- not
	have			have	

5. **Passivisation rule**

NP_1 - Aux. - V. - NP_2 **Pass.** ⟶ NP_2 - Aux. - **be - en** - V. - by - NP_1

COMPREHENSION QUESTIONS

1. What is TG Grammar? In what ways is it an improvement on the Structuralists' View of Grammar? Explain.
2. Explain what you mean by a Kernel sentence. Give examples.
3. Derive the following sentences from their Kernels:
   (a) Was she playing the match?
   (b) Has he signed the will?
   (c) May I come in?
   (d) How do you learn all this?
   (e) Why did you tell a lie?
   (f) Could you solve the puzzle?
   (g) What does Linguistics teach you?
   (h) Do you believe in God?
   (i) Did you win the game?
   (j) Who presided over the meeting?
4. Derive the following passive sentences from their Kernels:
   (a) He has been killed by the police.
   (b) My pen was stolen by him.
5. Write short notes on:
   (a) Passivisation.
   (b) Negativisation.

CHAPTER 11

Supra-sentential Grammar

11.1 INTRODUCTION

In Chapter 10, we considered some of the rules that make a sentence grammatical and meaningful. Now we may consider a higher level of language structure where two or more individual sentences may be related. These sentences make a larger unit of meaning that we call *text.* In other words, they are interrelated in such a way that they form a meaningful unit. This further corroborates that grammar and semantics are closely related. Meaning is created through lexical and grammatical devices which indicate connection between different units in a text.

11.2 SENTENCE CONNECTION

Sentence connection occurs through certain syntactic devices. Let us consider the following sentences:

The government felt that all boys and girls above the age of 18 should be given a definite role to shape the future of the country.

So they were given the right to vote.

The second sentence, we see, is a logical derivation of the first. It refers back to the first sentence and is thus connected to it. The word 'they' refers to "all boys and girls above the age of 18", which is a noun phrase in the earlier sentence. 'So' in the second sentence links it with the first sentence by showing that the second action "given the right to vote" is *a consequence* of the action in the first. The occurrence of 'so' is logical in the second sentence, not the first.

There are many such ways in which sentences are related and connected in this manner. To take another example, in the sentence immediately preceding this, we have used 'such'. What does 'such' refer to? Obviously, it relates to the point discussed in the previous paragraph. It is also a mode of sentence connection. It creates **cohesion,** which may be defined as a relationship between sentences in a text where the interpretation of some elements in one sentence depends on the elements in another. According to Halliday and Hasan (1976), cohesion is part of the system of a language expressed partly through grammar and partly through vocabulary.

11.3 COHESIVE DEVICES

The grammar of a language contains rules for sentence connection by using particular devices. Halliday and Hasan (*ibid.*) list these under the following categories:

• Reference • Substitution • Ellipsis • Conjunction • Lexical cohesion.

Let us first consider **conjunction**, which can be made through the following major cohesive devices:

1. *Time relators*

Time relationships between sentences can be signalled by adjectives and adverbials, which refer to events having occurred in succession to each other and thus establish a link between sentences:

(a) Adjectives such as **previous, earlier, former, preceding, following,** e.g. "His plan is excellent. The *previous* plan was poor". (Previous to the excellent plan). "He seemed to be in good health when I saw him on Friday. But *following* day he died". (that is, following the day mentioned in the first sentence).

(b) Adverbs such as **already, before, first, yet, now, so far, immediately, after, later, next, then,** etc., e.g. "I will give my comments. But *first* I must finish writing" (that is, before I give my comments). "He went to the board meeting this morning. He was *then* due to fly to London".

2. *Place relators*

These are words denoting place relationship to connect sentences: "He examined the car. The *front* was slightly damaged". (front of the car) "My friends have gone to Paris. I will go *there* next year." (to Paris)

3. *Additive conjuncts*

These indicate connection which adds to that which is given in the earlier sentence. For example, 'and' indicates addition, as do the phrases 'and also', 'further', 'besides', 'in addition'. 'Too' is another such conjunct, adding to what has been mentioned:

"The children read the play. They acted it *too*."

This category includes appositives: **'that is', 'for example', 'in other words'**. Another device is 'or' which can be an addition to what has been said indicating reformulation of the same statement, or one that offers an alternative to it., e.g. "You took the book without permission. (Or) In other words, you stole it." "You can take it. *Or* you can leave it."

This can be a negative addition, e.g. 'nor': 'They didn't read the play. *Nor* did they act it.'

4. *Adversative conjuncts*

These indicate opposition to the earlier statement, e.g. but, though, instead of, rather, however, despite, on the contrary, nevertheless.

5. *Causal conjuncts*

These denote result and consequence of what has been mentioned, e.g. then, hence, because, therefore, as a result. "They refused to pay the rent. *As a result,* they were evicted".

6. *Inferential conjuncts*

These indicate an inference which follows from that which has been mentioned, as 'in that case', 'if so': "He says he wants to marry Susan. If so, he shouldn't quarrel with her".

7. *Transitional conjuncts*

Occur in the middle of units to indicate a stage or transition, e.g. with regard to, speaking of, now, next: "I have discussed the points on the agenda. Now, do we need to discuss anything else"?

8. *Summative conjuncts*

Occur at the end of a unit of sum up the preceding statements: in brief, no conclude, in all.

9. *Ennumerative conjuncts*

These show the order of items in the form of listing, e.g. **First, second, further, finally, lastly, another**. There may be an indication of which items are more important, e.g. **above all, most significant (important), first and foremost**.

Some items indicate the attitude or orientation of the speaker. These attitudinal conjuncts are: **Surely, well, actually, after all.**

Let us now consider **Substitution.** Through substitution we can avoid repetition as well as abbreviate a sentence. These .substitutes are called **pro-forms,** and include pronominals (he, she, it, they, their, we, our) which substitute for noun phrases and their constituents. Examples are:

John was driving home. *His* car struck against a tree. *It* was badly damaged. *His* substitutes for John, *it* substitutes for car.

Other pro-forms are: one, all, any, some, none, both, neither, either, the same. They substitute for a noun phrase that has been mentioned earlier, as in the examples:

(a) Will you have coffee? Yes, I'll have *some.* (Substitutes for 'coffee')
(b) Do you have a pen? Yes, here's *one. (*Substitutes for 'pen')
(c) My friends have decided to go to the university. *None* of them are doing business. (Substitutes for 'my friends').

There are also pro-forms for predicates. The auxiliaries, 'do', 'have' and 'be', and modal auxiliaries substitute for the whole predicate phrase, as for example:

(a) John likes ice-cream. Mary *doesn't.*

(b) I've brought you a present. Oh, you shouldn't *have.*
(c) Can I go now? Yes, you *may.*
(d) She is a liar. No, she *can't be.*
(e) Some place-relators can be pro-forms, e.g. that, here, there:
(f) Let's meet for dinner tonight. *That* would be nice.
(g) Look for the book on the shelf. I put it *there.*

A negative pro-form for the predicate would be: *not.* Example: John is a coward. But *not* Bill. For an object clause, *so* becomes a substitute, e.g. I think our team will win the race. The coach told me *so.* (so = our team will win the race)

Ellipsis is a type of cohesion which is like substitution. Some parts of a sentence which have been stated earlier are omitted. The purpose is again to avoid repetition across sentences. Examples are:

(a) I'm a space explorer. Are you ( )? (element which undergoes ellipsis: a space explorer).
(b) When did he arrive? Probably ( ) last night. (element which undergoes ellipsis: he arrived).

Discourse reference. There are a number of items within a sentence that refer either backwards to what has been mentioned before in a previous sentence, in which case these items are **anaphoric,** or forwards to what is to be mentioned later, which are **cataphoric.** An example of anaphoric reference is: Many years ago their parents were sworn enemies. *That* is now forgotten. Their children are quite good friends. (*That* refers back to the statement given in the previous sentence.)

An example of cataphoric reference is: *Here* is the news. The President visited...(*Here* points forward to the next sentence.)

Pronouns are usually anaphoric. Items such as 'like', 'as follows' are cataphoric.

Taken together, anaphoric and cataphoric items create a unity of reference. By the use of these items it becomes clear as to what is being referred to, and thus a meaningful unit of discourse is created.

Lexical cohesion. This is of two types. The first type is *repetition* of the same lexical item in several sentences subsequent to its first occurrence, e.g. the word 'stone' repeated in several sentences after it has been used in the first sentence, The second type of lexical cohesion is *synonymy:* the use of synonyms or near-synonyms in subsequent sentences, e.g. if 'stone' is mentioned in the first sentence, subsequent sentences may mention 'rock', 'pebble', etc., and this creates cohesion since the reference is being made to the same or similar object.

There is **structural parallelism** between two sentences if they have an identical structure and also lexical cohesion or contrast, e.g. My painting they admired. My sculptures they disliked.' Though there is lexical contrast between 'admired' and 'disliked', the two sentences have similar structure of noun phrase beginning with 'my'.

Often, several of the cohesive devices described above are used in sentences, and these create sentence connection.

SUMMARY

Supra-sentential grammar consists of items which are used to make connections between sentences. They are also called *cohesive devices*. These are syntactic conjuncts: time relators, place-relators and logical connectors. Substitution, ellipsis and discourse reference are other types of intra-sentential connection. Lexical cohesion is achieved by use of synonyms, near-synonyms and antonyms.

COMPREHENSION QUESTIONS

1. Find and list all the cohesive devices used in the given passage: "With the progress of science, many relationships have been discovered between sunspots and things on earth and in the atmosphere. There are two main reasons for this. First, the scientist has developed more sensitive instruments for measuring solar radiations. But undoubtedly the main reason is the second one: over the last 40 years we have been studying the upper atmosphere, as distinct from the lower, and all kinds of phenomena have been discovered there which vary from the sunspot cycle."
2. Take some short texts and make a list of the types of sentence connection that you can find in them. You can take up a newspaper report, a prose narrative or literary piece.
3. Distinguish anaphoric and cataphoric reference in the following sentences:
   (a) When I was 18, I left my village. That was 15 years ago.
   (b) The above example is not correct. What follows is more appropriate.
   (c) The Chief is here. He arrived suddenly last night.
   (d) This is the position. We are under attack from all sides.
   (e) Fifty people voted against the resolution. The Committee had not forseen such opposition. They withdrew the resolution to plan their next move.

SECTION III

The Study of Semantics

CHAPTER 12

What is Semantics?

12.1 DEFINITION

Semantics is the study of meaning in language. We know that language is used to express meanings which can be understood by others. But meanings exist in our minds and we can express what is in our minds through the spoken and written forms of language (as well as through gestures, action etc.). The sound patterns of language are studied at the level of phonology and the organisation of words and sentences is studied at the level of morphology and syntax. These are in turn organised in such a way that we can convey meaningful messages or receive and understand messages. 'How is language organised in order to be meaningful?' This is the question we ask and attempt to answer at the level of semantics. Semantics is that level of linguistic analysis where meaning is analysed (see Section 2.4). It is the most abstract level of linguistic analysis, since we cannot see or observe meaning as we can observe and record sounds. Meaning is related very closely to the human capacity to think logically and to understand. So when we try to analyse meaning, we are trying to analyse our own capacity to think and understand, our own ability to create meaning. Semantics concerns itself with 'giving a systematic account of the nature of meaning' (Leech, 1981).

12.2 WHAT IS MEANING?

Philosophers have puzzled over this question for over 2000 years. Their thinking begins from the question of the relationship between words and the objects which words represent. For example, we may ask: What is the meaning of the word 'cow'? One answer would be that it refers to an animal who has certain properties, that distinguish it from other animals, who are called by other names. Where do these names come from and why does the word 'cow' mean only that particular animal and none other? Some thinkers say that there is no essential connection between the word 'cow' and the animal indicated by the word, but we have established this connection by convention and thus it continues to be so. Others would say that there are some essential attributes of that animal which we perceive in our minds and our concept of that animal is created for which we create a corresponding word. According to this idea, there is an essential correspondence between the sounds of words and their meanings, e.g., the word 'buzz' reproduces 'the sound made by a bee'. It is easy to understand this, but not so easy to understand how 'cow' can mean' a four-legged bovine'—there is nothing in the sound of the word 'cow' to indicate that, (Children often invent words that illustrate the correspondence between sound and meaning: they may call a cow 'moo-moo' because they hear it making that kind of sound.)

The above idea that words in a language correspond to or stand for the actual objects in the world is found in Plato's dialogue **Cratylus**. However, it applies only to some words and not to others, for example, words that do not refer to objects, e.g. 'love', 'hate'. This fact gives rise to the view held by later thinkers, that the meaning of a word is not the object it refers to, but the **concept** of the object that exists in the mind. Moreover, as de Saussure pointed out, the relation between the word (signifier) and the concept (signified) is an arbitrary one, i.e. the word does not resemble the concept (see Chapter 2). Also, when we try to define the meaning of a word we do so by using other words. So, if we try to explain the meaning of 'table' we need to use other words such as 'four', 'legs', and 'wood' and these words in turn can be explained only by means of other words.

In their book, *The Meaning of Meaning* (1923), L.K. Ogden and I.A. Richards made an attempt to define meaning. When we use the word 'mean', we use it in different ways. 'I mean to do this' is a way of expressing our intention. 'The red signal means stop' is a way of indicating what the red signal signifies. Since all language consists of signs, we can say that every word is a sign indicating something–usually a sign indicates other signs. Ogden and Richards give the following list of some definitions of 'meaning'. Meaning can be any of the following:

1. An intrinsic property of some thing
2. Other words related to that word in a dictionary
3. The connotations of a word (that is discussed below)
4. The thing to which the speaker of that word refers
5. The thing to which the speaker of that word **should** refer
6. The thing to which the speaker of that word believes himself to be referring
7. The thing to which the hearer of that word believes is being referred to.

These definitions refer to many different ways in which meaning is understood. One reason for the range of definitions of meaning is that words (or signs) in a language are of different types. Some signs indicate meaning in a direct manner, e.g. an arrow (⟶) indicates direction. Some signs are representative of the thing indicated, e.g. onomatopoeic words such as 'buzz', 'tinkle' 'ring'; even 'cough', 'slam', 'rustle' have onomatopoeic qualities. Some signs do not have any resemblance to the thing they refer to, but as they stand for that thing, they are symbolic.

Taking up some of the above definitions of meaning, we can discuss the different aspects of meaning of a word as follows:

1. *The logical or denotative meaning*

This is the literal meaning of a word indicating the **idea** or concept to which it refers. The concept is a minimal unit of meaning which could be called a '**sememe**' in the same way as the unit of sound is called a 'phoneme' and is like the 'morpheme' in its structure and organi-sation. Just as the phoneme /b/ may be defined as a bilabial + voiced + plosive, the word 'man' may be defined as a concept consisting of a structure of meaning 'human + male + adult' expressed through the basic morphological unit 'm + æ + n'. All the three qualities are logical attributes of which the concept 'man' is made. They are the minimal qualities that the concept must possess in order to be a distinguishable concept, e.g. if any of these changes, the concept too changes. So 'human + female + adult' would not be the concept referred to by the word 'man', since it is a different concept.

2. *The connotative meaning*

This is the additional meaning that a concept carries. It is defined as 'the communicative value an expression has by virtue of what it refers to over and above its purely conceptual content' (Leech, 1981). That is, apart from its logical or essential attributes, there is a further meaning attached to a word, which comes from its reference to other things in the real world. In the real world, such a word may be associated with some other features or attributes. For example, the logical or denotative meaning of the word 'woman' is the concept, 'human + female + adult'. To it may be added the concept of 'weaker sex' or 'frailty'. These were the connotations or values associated with the concept of 'woman'. Thus connotative meaning consists of the attributes associated with a concept. As we know, these associations come into use over a period of time in a particular culture and can change with change in time. While denotative meaning remains stable since it defines the essential attributes of a concept, connotative meaning changes as it is based on associations made to the concept; these associations may change.

3. *The social meaning*

This is the meaning that a word or a phrase conveys about the circumstances of its use. That is, the meaning of a word is understood according to the different style and situation in which the word is used, e.g. though the words 'domicile', 'residence', 'abode', 'home' all refer to the same thing (i.e. their denotative meaning is the same), each word belongs to a particular situation of use—'domicile' is used in an official context, 'residence' in a formal context, 'abode' is a poetic use and 'home' is an ordinary use. Where one is used, the other is not seen as appropriate. Social meaning derives from an awareness of the style in which something is written and spoken and of the relationship between speaker and hearer—whether that relationship is formal, official, casual, polite, or friendly.

4. *The thematic meaning*

This is the meaning which is communicated by the way in which a speaker or writer organises the message in terms of ordering, focus and emphasis. It is often felt, for example, that an active sentence has a different meaning from its passive equivalent although its conceptual meaning seems to be the same. In the sentences:

Mrs. Smith donated the first prize
The first prize was donated by Mrs. Smith

the thematic meaning is different. In the first sentence it appears that we know who Mrs. Smith is, so the new information on which the emphasis is laid is 'the first prize'. In the second sentence, however, the emphasis is laid on 'Mrs. Smith'.

It is sometimes difficult to demarcate all these categories of meaning. For example, it may be difficult to distinguish between conceptual meaning and social meaning in the following sentences:

He **stuck** the key in his pocket.
He **put** the key in his pocket.

We could argue that these two sentences are conceptually alike, but different in social meaning—the first one adopts a casual or informal style, the second adopts a neutral style. However, we could also say that the two verbs are conceptually different: 'stuck' meaning 'put carelessly and quickly', which is a more precise meaning than simply 'put'. Of course, it is a matter of choice which word the speaker wishes to use, a more precise one or a neutral one.

12.3 SOME TERMS AND DISTINCTIONS IN SEMANTICS

12.31 Lexical and Grammatical Meaning

Lexical or word meaning is the meaning of individual lexical items. These are of two types: the open class lexical items, such as nouns, verbs, adjectives and adverbs, and the close class items such as prepositions, conjunctions and determiners. The open class items have independent meanings, which are defined in the dictionary. The closed class items have meaning only in relation to other words in a sentence; this is called **grammatical** meaning, which can be understood from a consideration of the structure of the sentence and its relation with other sentences. For example, in the sentence 'The tiger killed the elephant', there are three open class items: tiger, kill, elephant. Out of these, two are nouns and one is a verb. There is one closed class item—'the'—which occurs before each noun. It has no independent reference of its own and can have meaning only when placed before the nouns.

This distinction may help in understanding ambiguity. Thus, if there is ambiguity in a sentence, this can be a lexical ambiguity or a grammatical ambiguity. For example, in the sentence:

I saw him near the bank.

there is lexical ambiguity, since the item 'bank' can mean (a) the financial institution or (b) the bank of a river. However, in the case of:

'The parents of the bride and the groom were waiting' there is grammatical ambiguity as the sentence structure can be interpreted in two ways: (a) the two separate noun phrases being 'the parents of the bride', and 'the groom'; or (b) the single noun phrase 'the parents' within which there is the prepositional phrase 'of the bride and the groom' containing two nouns. The first type of coordination gives us the meaning that the people who were waiting were the parents of the bride and the groom himself. The second type of coordination gives us the meaning that the people who were waiting were the parents of the bride and the parents of the groom.

The meaning of a sentence is the product of both lexical and grammatical meanings. This becomes clear if we compare a pair of sentences such as the following:

The dog bit the postman.
The postman bit the dog.

These two sentences differ in meaning. But the difference in meaning is not due to the difference in the meaning of the lexical items 'postman' and 'dog', but in the grammatical relationship between the two. In one case 'dog' is the subject and 'postman' is the object, in the other case the grammatical roles are reversed. There is also the relationship of these nouns with the verb 'bit'. In the first sentence, the action is performed by the dog, which conforms to our knowledge about dogs, but in the second sentence, the action is performed by the postman which does not match with our knowledge about what postmen do, so there is a sense of incongruity about the second sentence. Only in some exceptional circumstance could we expect it to be comprehensible.

12.32 Sense and Reference

It has been explained earlier that signs refer to concepts as well as to other signs. A sign is a symbol that indicates a concept. This concept is the reference, which refers in turn to some object in the real world, called the referent. The relationship between linguistic items (e.g. words, sentences) and the non-linguistic world of experience is a relationship of reference. It can be understood by the following diagram given by Ogden and Richards (1923):

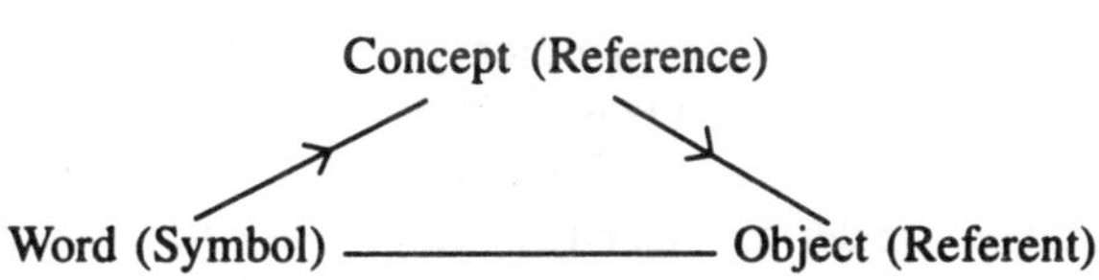

The objects in the real world are **referents**, the concept which we have of them in our minds is the **reference** and the symbol we use to refer to them is the **word**, or linguistic item.

As we have seen, we can explain the meaning of a linguistic item by using other words. The relation of a word with another word is a **sense-relation**. Therefore, sense is the complex system of relationships that holds between the linguistic items themselves. Sense is concerned with the intra-linguistic relations, i.e. relations within the system of the language itself, such as similarity between words, opposition, inclusion, and pre-supposition.

Sense relations include homonymy, polysemy, synonymy and antonymy. **Homonyms** are different items (lexical items or structure words) with the same phonetic form. They differ only in meaning, e.g. the item 'ear' meaning 'organ of hearing' is a homonym of the item 'ear' meaning 'a stem of wheat'. Homonymy may be classified as:

(a) Homography: a phenomenon of two or more words having the **same spellings** but different pronunciation or meaning, e.g. lead/led/ = metal; lead/li:d/ = verb.
(b) Homophony: a phenomenon of two or more words having the **same pronunciation** but different meanings or spellings, e.g. sea/see, knew/new, some/sum, sun/son.

It is difficult to distinguish between homonymy and polysemy as in **polysemy**, the 'same' lexical item has different meanings, e.g. 'bank*', 'face*': Two lexical items can be considered as **synonyms** if they have the same denotative, connotative and social meaning and can replace each other in all contexts of occurrence. Only then can they be absolutely synonymous. For example, 'radio' and 'wireless' co-existed for a while as synonyms, being used as alternatives by speakers of British English. But now, 'wireless' is not used frequently. What we consider as synonyms in a language are usually near-equivalent items, or descriptive items. For example, 'lavatory', 'toilet', 'WC', 'washroom' are descriptive or near-equivalent synonyms in English.

Antonyms are lexical items which are different both in form as well as meaning. An antonym of a lexical item conveys the opposite sense, e.g. single-married, good-bad. But this gives rise to questions of what is an opposite or contrasted meaning. For example, the opposite of 'woman' could be 'man' or 'girl' since the denotation of both is different from that of 'woman'. Thus we need to modify our definition of antonymy. We can say that some items are less compatible than other items. There can be nearness of contrast or remoteness of contrast. Thus 'man' or 'girl' is contrasted to 'woman' but less contrasted than 'woman' and 'tree'. In this sense, 'woman' and 'man' are related, just as 'girl' and 'boy' are related, in spite of being contrasted. Other meaning-relations of a similar nature are: mare/stallion, cow/bull, **ram/ewe** etc., all based on gender distinctions. Another set of meaning relations can be of age and family relationship: father/son, uncle/nephew, aunt/niece. In this, too, there are differences in the structures of different languages. In Hindi, for instance, gender distinction or contrast may be marked by a change in the ending of the noun (e.g. /gho:ɽɑ/gho:ɽi:/ for 'horse' and 'mare' respectively) or, in some cases, by a different word (e.g. /gɑ:e/bɑel/ for 'cow' and 'bull' respectively). In English, there are usually different words to mark contrast in gender except in a few cases (e.g. elephant, giraffe). The evolution of a complex system of sense relations is dependent on the way in which the objects of the

* bank^1 = a financial institution
bank^2 = bank of a river
bank^3 = a row of keys
bank^4 = as verb
* face^1 = front part of head
face^2 = expression on face
face^3 = surface or side

world and the environment are perceived and conceptualized by the people who make that language. For example, Eskimos have many words related in meaning to 'snow' because snow in different forms is a part of their environment. In English, there are only two 'snow' and 'ice', while in Hindi there is only one: 'baraf'. This reflects the importance that a particular object or phenomena may have for a certain community.

Another kind of sense-relationship is **hyponymy**. Hyponymy is the relation that holds between a more general and more specific lexical item. For example, 'flower' is a more general item, and 'rose', 'lily', etc. are more specific. The more specific item is considered a hyponym of the more general item—'rose' is a hyponym of 'flower'. The specific item includes the meaning of the general. When we say 'rose', the meaning of 'flower' is included in its meaning. 'Rose' is also hyponymous to 'plant' and 'living thing' as these are the most general categories.

The combination of words to produce a single unit of meaning is also a part of sense-relations in a language. Compounds are made, which often do not mean the same as the separate words which they consist of. Thus, while 'black bird' can be understood to mean 'a bird which is black', 'strawberry' cannot be understood to mean 'a berry made of straw'. Similarly, 'fighter' can be considered to be a noun made up of the morphemes 'fight' + 'er', but 'hammer' cannot be considered as made up of 'ham' + 'er'. Phrasal verbs and idioms are also a case of such sense relations. The verbs 'face up to', 'see through', 'look upon', etc. have a composite meaning. Collocations such as 'heavy smoker' and 'good singer' are not mere combinations of heavy + smoker meaning 'the smoker is heavy' or 'good + singer'. They mean 'one who smokes heavily' or 'one who sings well'. The collocated unit has a meaning which is a composite of both that is why we cannot say 'good smoker' and 'heavy singer'. All these sense-relations are peculiar to a language and every language develops its own system of sense-relations.

12.33 Sentence-meaning and Utterance-meaning

A distinction may be drawn between sentence-meaning and utterance-meaning. This is because a speaker may use a sentence to mean something other than what is normally stated in the sentence itself. As discussed earlier, sentence meaning is a combination of lexical and grammatical meaning. In addition to this, intonation may also affect sentence meaning. For example, 'I don't like **COFFEE**' means that the speaker does not like coffee, but may like some other drink; '**I** don't like coffee' means that the speaker doesn't like coffee but someone else does. Speakers can use intonation to change the emphasis and thus the meaning of the sentence.

Further, a sentence may be used by a speaker to perform some act, such as the act of questioning, warning, promising, threatening, etc. Thus, a sentence such as 'Its cold in here' could be used as an order or request to someone to shut the window, even though it is a declarative sentence. Similarly, an interrogative sentence such as 'Could you shut the door?' can be used to perform the act of requesting or commanding rather than that of questioning (The speaker is not asking whether the hearer is able to shut the door, but is requesting the hearer to actually do the action). Usually such use of sentences is so conventional that we do not stop to think of the literal sentence meaning, we respond to the speaker's act of requesting, etc., which is the utterance meaning. This is the meaning that a sentence has when a speaker utters it to perform some act, in particular appropriate circumstances.

12.34 Entailment and Presupposition

One sentence may entail other sentence—that is, include the meaning of other sentence in its meaning, just as hyponymy includes the meaning of other word. For example, the sentence 'The earth goes round the sun' entails (includes) the meaning 'The earth moves'.

A sentence may presuppose other sentences, e.g. the sentence 'Shiva's son is named Ganesh' presupposes the sentence 'Shiva has a son'. Presupposition is the previously known meaning which is implied in the sentence. While entailment is a logical meaning inherent in the sentence, presupposition may depend on the knowledge of the facts, shared by the speaker and the hearer. We may go on exploring further aspects of the study of meaning by a consideration of some theories of semantics in Chapter 12.

SUMMARY

Semantics is the study of meaning in language. It is the level at which we attempt to analyse how meanings are expressed and understood. The first problem is that of defining meaning.

Meaning lies in the relationship between words and the concepts for which these words stand. These relationships can be of various types. Some of these types of meaning are:

(i) ***Denotative meaning.*** The logical meaning, which indicates the essential qualities of a concept which distinguish it from other concepts.

(ii) ***Connotative meaning.*** The additional or associated meaning, which is attached to the denotative, conceptual meaning. It consists of associations made with a concept whenever that concept is referred to.

(iii) ***Social meaning.*** It is the meaning that a word possesses by virtue of its use in particular social situations and circumstances.

(iv) ***Thematic meaning.*** It lies in the manner in which a message is organised for emphasis.

Some important distinctions are made in semantics between the following:

1. ***Lexical and grammatical meaning.*** This is the distinction between word meaning and sentence meaning, i.e. the meaning of individual lexical items as distinct from the meaning which they have in combination with other items in a sentence.

2. ***Sense and reference.*** While reference is the indication of relationship between a word and a concept or object in the external world, sense is the internal relationship of the word with other words. Sense relations include relations of synonymy (similar meaning), hyponymy (inclusion of the meaning of one within the other), antonymy (opposite meaning) and homonymy (similar sound, different meaning).

3. ***Sentence and utterance.*** Sentence is the grammatical unit which contains a logical statement or proposition, utterance is the speaking or writing of a sentence by a user, in a context.

4. ***Entailment and presupposition.*** One sentence entails another when it includes the meaning of the other sentence. One sentence presupposes another when it implies an earlier meaning which is known.

COMPREHENSION QUESTIONS

1. Make a chart showing hyponyms of the following words: tree; meat; vegetable; fruit (e.g. meat has hyponyms such as: beef, pork, chicken, and mutton).
2. Consult a thesaurus and pick out the synonyms of the following words, taking care that only the words which are nearest in meaning and can be used in the same context are chosen: silent, descend, record, shop, bad.
3. Discuss entailment and presupposition in the following sentences:
   (a) John's father lives in New York.
   (b) The athlete won the race.
4. Discuss some examples of sense-relations in the semantic structure of your own language. Suggest some collocations which are unique in your language.

CHAPTER 13

Theories of Semantics

13.1 VIEWS OF MEANING

As in the case of grammar, many explanations of meaning and attempts to analyse meaning in language have been made by linguists. The structural linguists were of the view that meaning cannot be studied as part of the scope of linguistics since linguistics studies language as a hierarchical structure of systems such as phonology, morphology and syntax. The purpose of language study is to describe this hierarchical structure. However, an attempt was made by structuralists to describe meaning in a scientific manner by breaking up the meanings of words into distinct elements. This approach will be discussed in detail below.

Meaning can be studied as a part of linguistics since meaning is a part of language and not independent of language. There is no escape from language and it is a fundamental tool for expression of meaning. Also, every language builds up a system of meaning based on concepts and relationships between concepts. Sense-relations and references are thus created. This becomes a level of organisation or system within the language itself, in the same way as phonology and syntax. Thus, a semanticist (like a phonologist or grammarian) is concerned with a description of the meaning of words, sentences etc. and with the manner in which the meaning of these words and sentences is used and understood. Knowing a language involves recognizing the relation of meaning between words and sentences and recognizing which words and sentences are meaningful and which are not. The native speaker of a language has a 'semantic competence' which helps in recognizing that certain utterances—whether they are words or sentences—are not meaningful even if they obey the grammatical rules of the language. For example, the sentence 'colourless green ideas sleep furiously' or a word such as 'gimble' or 'wabe' are recognized as meaningless. But we need to understand why this is so. The semanticist attempts to analyse the reasons why such utterances are not meaningful.

This can be understood in two ways. An utterance is meaningless either because it is not logical in some way, or because it violates some rules of lexical or grammatical combination. There is a close relation between language and logic. We cannot accept a sentence as meaningful if it is illogical and does not communicate anything. For example, in the sentence:

Monday came before the day which followed it.

This is a circular statement which tells us nothing. Such statements are called tautological statements. Then there are contradictory statements, which are false in meaning, e.g.

'My unmarried sister is married to a bachelor'.

We know this cannot be true—a person cannot be both married and unmarried, and a bachelor cannot be married. Thus this statement is absurd. Another kind of absurdity is apparent in:

My uncle always sleeps standing on one toe.

We know this cannot be true, because it does not correspond to what we know about the real world. This kind of absurdity is called factual absurdity. While we can resolve this kind of absurdity by imagining a possible world in which it could be true, we cannot resolve a contradiction unless we change the sentence itself.

As some explanations or theories of semantics are based on the structuralist approach, some are based on logic, and some on the generative approach. Some give an account of word meaning whereas others attempt to account for sentence meaning.

13.2 THE COMPONENTIAL THEORY OF MEANING

This theory based on the structural approach gives an account of word meaning. The total meaning of a word is broken up into its basic distinct components. Each component of meaning is expressed by a feature symbol with a + or – mark to indicate the presence or absence of a certain feature. In the following we can consider some features as:

HUMAN	:	+ Human (human being)
		– Human (animal)
ADULT	:	+ ADULT (adult)
		– ADULT (young)
MALE	:	+ MALE (male)
		– MALE (female)

Subsequently the meanings of some individual words can be expressed by the combinations of these features:

Man	:	+ HUMAN + ADULT + MALE
Woman	:	+ HUMAN + ADULT – MALE
Boy	:	+ HUMAN – ADULT + MALE
Girl	:	+ HUMAN – ADULT – MALE

The meaning of each word is understood as a combination of these ultimate contrastive elements. It may be noted that componential analysis of this kind treats components in terms of binary opposites, i.e. '+' and '–' features. However, this works only where there is a clear distinction, that of male vs. female, human vs. animal, married vs. unmarried. It can help us to bring out the logical features which are inherent in a word, and thus exclude some meanings, for example, if we characterise 'bachelor' as '+male, –married', the meaning of 'married bachelor' can be excluded.

Componential analysis helps us understand meaning relations such as synonymy and antonymy. These can be understood as meaning inclusion (including of similar meanings being similarity relation) and meaning exclusion (contrasting relations). Two componential meanings are exclusive if one contains at least one feature contrasting with one feature of the other. Thus the meaning of 'woman' is opposite or contrasted to that of 'child' because of the contrast between the features + ADULT and – ADULT in these two words:

Woman = + HUMAN + ADULT – MALE
Child = + HUMAN – ADULT – MALE
or + MALE

The meaning of 'woman' contrasts with the meaning of 'man', as also with the meaning of 'child'. While + ADULT is hyponymous to 'woman' and 'man' (i.e. 'adult' includes both 'woman' and 'man'), it is incompatible with 'child' ('+ adult' is excluded from the meaning of 'child').

While many meanings can be understood in terms of binary contrasts, there are some oppositions that involve more than two terms. Examples are in the field of description of species of animals or plants, types of metals, colours, etc. Thus, all metals—gold, silver, copper, etc. are different types of metal, though they are all '+ METAL'. Similarly, not only do we have different colours, e.g. red, brown, but also descriptive names for transitional shades of colours for instance, reddish-brown, brownish red. Giving these examples, Leech (1981) calls them instances of **multiple taxonomy**.

In addition to these, there are instances of contrasts between some antonyms, e.g. rich/poor, old/young, deep/shallow, in which we can have various stages between the two extremes. Thus, while we cannot say 'John is married and unmarried' or 'The man is neither dead nor alive' as these statements would be contradictory, we can say 'The man is neither rich nor poor'; meaning that there is an intermediate stage between 'rich' and 'poor'. This kind of meaning also brings in a degree of relativity—we can say 'rich' or 'poor', 'good' or 'bad' in relation to some norm which may be specific for a speaker or a situation. For example, both statements 'London is beautiful' and 'London is ugly' could be consistent because one could be true for one person and the other for another person.

In relations too, there can be cases where the opposite is entailed and cases where it is not. For example, we can say 'Ram is married to Sita' which entails 'Sita is married to Ram'. This is a symmetric relation. However, if we say 'Ram is the father of Mohan' we cannot assume the opposite. This is an asymmetric relation.

These are some of the basic methods of componential analysis of meaning. These are helpful in making conceptual distinctions and contrasts for the understanding of the meaning. However, they do not explain what are called 'fuzzy meanings', i.e. those meanings that are more vague and in which there is less agreement and certainty about the exact nature of objects and concepts. For example, there are many attributes that determine whether we can call something a cup, but these attributes vary in importance. 'Cup' cannot be defined in terms of a clear-cut, unvarying set of attributes (e.g. with/without handle, narrow/wide, deep/shallow) since there are so many different types of cups. Therefore 'cup' can be defined only in terms of 'fuzzy sets' of attributes.

13.3 TRUTH-CONDITIONAL THEORY OF MEANING

This theory takes up the account of meaning of sentences. According to Leech (1983, p. 73):

> Many semanticists today assume that the main purpose of semantics is to explain that primary, conceptual aspect of meaning called 'conceptual' or 'logical' meaning, and that in particular we have to account for certain semantic categories and relationships which apply to sentences: synonymy, entailment, contradiction, semantic anomaly etc. These may be taken to be intuitively 'given'. They can be called BASIC STATEMENTS... because semantics has to explain them, by constructing theories from which they can be deduced.

The basic statement is a logical proposition which is either TRUE or FALSE. Its truth or falsity is dependent or conditional upon the truth or falsity of other statements. For example, we have a sentence 'John is in his office'. This statement will be true if the statement 'John is at home' is false. Basic statements relate to other statements in terms of the following:

(i) Synonymy. Statement X is synonymous with statement Y when if X is true, Y is also true; if X is false, Y is also false. Thus 'He is married' is synonymous with 'He has a wife'.

(ii) Entailment. Statement X entails statement Y when if X is true, Y is true; if X is false, Y is false. 'He is married' entails 'He has a wife'. (Entailment and synonymy are similar.)

(iii) Inconsistent. Statement X is inconsistent with statement Y when if X is true, Y is false; if Y is true, X is false. 'He is not married' is inconsistent with 'He has a wife'.

(iv) Tautology. Statement X is invariably true, e.g. An orphan has no father.

(v) Contradiction. Statement X is invariably false, e.g. An orphan has a father.

(vi) Presupposition. Statement X presupposes statement Y when if X is true, Y is true; if negation of X is true, Y is true. 'It pleases John that the weather is hot' presupposes 'the weather is hot'.

(vii) Anomaly or Absurdity. Statement X is absurd in that it presupposes a contradiction, e.g. 'The orphan's father is at home' presupposes that 'The orphan has a father' which is a contradiction, and is therefore absurd.

A native speaker of a language can infer the truth of propositions in that language from the truth of other propositions. The speaker knows the conditions in which a particular sentence is true. Thus, according to truth-conditional semantics, to know the meaning of a sentence is to know the conditions under which it is true. A sentence is true if all the necessary conditions of truth are satisfied. These conditions do not refer to the real world, they are conditional within the language, i.e. within the entailment relations that prevail between sentences. Thus: 'Rover is a hungry dog' is true if 'Rover is a dog' and 'Rover is hungry' are both true. The first statement entails the other two.

The goal of truth-conditional semantics is to explain meaning by explaining all the entailment relations between sentences in the language. One of the limitations of this approach is that it takes only statements into account and does not consider other sentence-types such as questions. Some semanticists say that even questions have a basis in conditions of truth as they can elicit either a positive proposition ('Yes') or a negative proposition ('No') in reply. Another limitation is that truth-conditional semantics is not concerned with synthetic truth, i.e. factual truth about the conditions which prevail in the real world; it is concerned about analytic truth, i.e. truth by the very nature of language, e.g. entailment relations between sentences, as discussed above. For instance, the statement 'All bachelors are unmarried' is true because the very definition of 'bachelor' is 'being unmarried'. This relation exists within the language. But in the sentence 'All bachelors are happy', the truth does not lie in the language but in some conditions outside it, in the real world. Truth-conditional semantics thus explains the meaning of sentences to a limited extent, but does so in a logical and scientific manner.

13.4 GENERATIVE THEORY OF MEANING

The study of meaning became the subject of renewed interest with the development of the transformational-generative model of grammar. This model sought to relate meaning with syntax and sound through a set of transformations from deep structure to surface structure. Chomsky's Standard Theory and the later Revised Extended Standard Theory is based on the notion that the deep structure of a sentence and the meanings of words (lexical items) used in that structure represent the total meaning of the sentence. At the level of deep structure, lexical items are inserted into syntactic forms, with the application of 'selection restrictions', and concepts such as subject and object are defined. Selection restrictions are rules regarding the permissible combination of lexical items in language. These rules prevent the generation of unmeaningful or anomalous sentences such as 'colourless green ideas sleep furiously' or combinations such as 'red hope'. Restrictions are also placed at the level of deep structure on the choice of certain grammatical items in relation to other grammatical items, e.g. the rule must indicate whether a verb is transitive or not if it is to have a noun phrase after it in the syntactic structure, so that the sentence 'The man died' can be generated but not the sentence 'The man killed', unless there is a noun phrase after 'killed'. Similarly, 'frightened' and 'scared' are verbs both of which contain the meaning of fear, and have the same selection restrictions, i.e., 'The idea frightened the girl' and 'The idea scared the girl' are both acceptable, but neither 'The girl frightened the idea' nor 'The girl scared the idea' are acceptable. Therefore, 'scared' and 'frightened' are synonyms. The semantic information contained in some lexical items determines their role in the sentence. Verbs like 'talk', 'dream', etc. contain the information '+human', so that they cannot have a subject such as, 'iron'. The adjective 'red' carries a specification of '+ concrete', e.g. 'red book', and therefore cannot be used for an object with a '– concrete' feature, for example, 'red hope' is not permissible. The specific properties of each lexical item along with the knowledge of rules regarding the selection of the item are present in the internalized dictionary or lexicon of a language which every native speaker possesses.

13.5 CONTEXTUAL THEORIES OF MEANING

In recent years, some theories have been developed which deal with the meanings of words and sentences not as isolated entities but as related to situations of occurrence and use. One such theory is the **Field Theory** developed in Europe by Trier. It explains the vocabulary or lexicon of a language as a system of inter-related networks or semantic fields. Words that are inter-related may belong to the same semantic field, e.g. 'flower', 'bloom', 'blossom', 'bud', belong to the same field. There may be overlapping between fields, e.g. the field of 'flower' and 'tree' may overlap in relation to such as 'plant', 'grow'. This is also the basis of the idea of collocation, since collocated items are those which habitually co-occur with certain other items, e.g. 'flowers' collocate with 'bloom', 'letters' with 'writing'. These networks and collocations are built on sense relations in a language.

Other contextual theories deal with the context of use of words and sentences by the speakers of a language. A term given by Firth (1957) is 'context of situation', in which meaning is related on the one hand to the external world or situation and on the other to levels of language such as the sounds, syntax and words. When we try to analyse the meaning of a word or sentence, the set of features from the external world or the 'context of situation' becomes relevant, i.e. who is the speaker, who is the hearer, what is the role of each and the relationship of the two, what situation they are in. According to Firth, language is only meaningful in the context of situation. This idea becomes the basis of the link between syntax and meaning-in-context which has recently been developed in Halliday's functional approach (1978). Grammaticality is linked to appropriacy in this approach, since the meaning of the sentence is understood according to the real world context, the participants, etc. For example, the sentence 'It's raining cats and dogs' is grammatical, but will not be meaningful if (a) it is not actually raining and (b) the speaker is making a formal speech. The context of situation refers to the situation of discourse, i.e. the context in which that particular sentence is uttered.

The notion of contextual appropriacy and the fact that the utterance of an item of language is an act performed by speakers, has led to the development of the theories of **pragmatics**, which will be considered in the next chapter.

SUMMARY

Semantics is the level of linguistic analysis at which meaning can be analysed. We can attempt to understand what makes words, sentences and utterances meaningful, or what makes them meaningless. If an utterance is not logical, it is meaningless, i.e. if it is tautological (circular, not communicating anything) or if it is contradictory (a false statement), it cannot be meaningful. Also, if a statement does not correspond to real world knowledge, it can be absurd.

Certain approaches in semantics enable us to describe meaning in a more precise and scientific manner. Componential theory gives an account of meaning in which the meaning of a word can be split up into its component parts. Each part is marked by the presence or absence of certain features (e.g. '+ human' or '– human') that contrast it from other words. We can make a table of binary contrasts to distinguish the meaning of one word from another, listing all the component parts. Truth-conditional semantics attempts to explain the logical meaning of sentences, treating a sentence as a logical proposition or basic statement which can be either true or false. It holds that if we know the conditions under which a particular sentence is true, we can infer the truth of related propositions. It does not refer to the external world, but to the logical relations existing between propositions. Generative theory deals with meaning as deep structure, where lexical items with particular features are selected to combine with others to generate a meaningful sentence. Contextual theory describes meaning in contexts of occurrence and use, e.g. when some item is regularly associated with another item in collocation.

COMPREHENSION QUESTIONS

1. Explain why the following sentences are not meaningful:
   (a) The stones ate food.
   (b) The bachelor gave birth to a baby.
   (c) The girl is happily unhappy.
   (d) Laughing mattresses jingled with joy.
2. Make a chart listing the componential features of:
   Family
   Tree
   Book
   Hope
3. Which of the following collocations are acceptable and which are not: pretty boy, suave woman, rancid butter, stale news, clever hope, fresh work.

CHAPTER 14

Semantics, Pragmatics and Discourse

14.1 SEMANTICS AND PRAGMATICS

Not only has semantics now become an important area of inquiry in linguistics, but it has also been extended to the level of pragmatics. Pragmatics is seen by some linguists as an independent level of language analysis as it is based on utterances in the same way as phonology is based on sound, syntax on sentences and semantics on both words and sentences. The link between pragmatics and semantics remains, however, that at both levels we are concerned with meaning. Semantics attempts to relate meaning to logic and truth, and deals with meaning as a matter primarily of sense-relations within the language. Pragmatics attempts to relate meaning to context of utterance; it views language as action which is performed by speakers.

What is the context of utterance? A sentence is uttered by a speaker, and when the speaker utters it, he/she performs an act. This is called a **speech-act**. Since it is performed by a speaker in relation to a hearer (or addressee), it depends on the conditions prevailing at the time the speech-act is performed. These conditions include the previous knowledge shared by speaker and hearer, and the reasons for the performance of the act. All these taken together constitute the context of utterance-speaker(s), hearer(h), sentence(s) and utterance(u).

Meaning in this sense involves the speaker's intention to convey a certain meaning which may not be evident in the message itself. In the sentence 'There's a fly in my soup', the message is that 'There is a fly in my soup' in which the speaker's intention may be to complain. So the meaning of the utterance contains the meaning of complaint. A hearer hearing this sentence may interpret it not just as a statement but as a request to take the soup away. That is, the meaning will include some intended effect on the hearer.

The consideration of meaning as a part of the utterance or speech act was initiated by the philosopher J.L. Austin (*How to Do Things With Words,* 1960) and developed by J. Searle and H.P. Grice. Let us consider Austin's idea first. Keeping in view the above distinction between the speaker's intention to convey a particular meaning which may not be evident in the message itself, Austin makes a distinction between **Sense** and **Force**. Sense is the propositional content or logical meaning of a sentence. Austin calls it the **locutionary** meaning. Force is the act performed in uttering a sentence. It is the performative meaning, defined by Austin as **Illocutionary Force**. For example, the utterance 'Please shut the door' is an imperative sentence. The logical or propositional context is that of shutting the door. It will have the force of request if the speaker and hearer are in some relationship which allows the speaker to make requests to the hearer, the hearer is in a position where he is capable of shutting the door, there is a particular door which the speaker is indicating and that door is open. If all these conditions are not fulfilled, the utterance will not have the force of request. We can chart the meaning of the above sentence as follows:

Please shut the door	Sentence form : Imperative
	Sense : Shutting the door (someone)
	Force : Request

In this sentence, sense and force are very similar to each other. However, in some cases there may be a difference. For example, if the speaker says, 'Can you shut the door?' the sentence form is interrogative, the sense is 'can' + 'you' + 'shut the door', that is, the logical meaning of the sentence is a question about the ability of the hearer to shut the door, evident in the sense of the modal 'can'. However, the force is still that of request. In such an utterance, it is clear that the sense is not the total meaning of the utterance, and that if only the sense is considered, the utterance will not succeed as a successful communication. If the hearer takes only the sense of the above sentence, he will understand the sentence only as a question regarding his ability to shut the door; it is only when the force of the utterance is understood that the hearer takes it as a request to shut the door, provided all the conditions for the performance of the request are fulfilled.

In other instances there is even more discrepancy between what the sentence says and what the speaker of the sentence intends the hearer to understand by it, i.e. between sense and force. 'There's a cold breeze coming through the door' is a statement in terms of form and sense, but the speaker may intend it to be a request to shut the door. In this way, there can be any number of variable meanings of the same utterance.

This raises a problem: how can we interpret a sentence when sense and force are very different and nothing in the sentence itself indicates what its force can be? Here a distinction can be made between utterances which are more conventional in nature and others which are more individual and situation-specific. For example, 'Can you shut the door?' is the kind of utterance which has become conventionalized to a great extent, so that a hearer is less likely to misinterpret it as a real question, and more likely to understand its force of request. But in the case of 'There's a cold breeze coming through the door', or 'Its very cold in the room' or 'Are you immune to cold?', there is a more indirect manner of making the request to the hearer. These are more dependent on the relation between the speaker and the hearer. While the conventionalized utterance can occur in many situations, the variable utterances can occur only in specific situations e.g. informal, friendly etc. Only under such conditions will the hearer be able to infer the intended meaning of the speaker.

It is for this reason that Grice (*Logic and Conversation*, 1975) explains that all communication takes place in a situation where people are co-operative. When people communicate, they assume that the other person will be cooperative and they themselves wish to cooperate. Grice calls this the "Cooperative Principle". Under this principle, the following maxims are followed:

(i) Maxim of quantity. Give the right amount of information, neither less nor more than what is required.

(ii) Maxim of quality. Make your contribution such that it is true; do not say what you know is false or for which you do not have adequate evidence.

(iii) Maxim of relation. Be relevant.

(iv) Maxim of manner. Avoid obscurity and ambiguity; be brief and orderly.

These 'Maxims' are different from rules in that while rules cannot be violated, maxims are often violated. That is, people often give more or less information than required, or make irrelevant contributions. When this happens, some implied meanings arise as a result. For example, in the interaction:

A : Where's my box of chocolates?
B : The children were in your room this morning (taken from Leech, 1981).

B violates the Maxim of relation because the reply is apparently not relevant to A's question. A proper response to A's question would be that B answers A's question about where the chocolates are. Since B does not give this answer, it implies that B does not know the answer, and also implies a suggestion on B's part that the children may have taken the chocolates. Similarly, in the interaction:

A : I failed in my test today.
B : Wonderful!

In this case, B's response violates the maxim of quality in that the expression 'wonderful' here is not an expression of delight or actual wonder. A's statement is not such that would demand a response of exclamation of delight. That such a response is given by B means that B implies something else: the negative of 'wonderful' meaning 'its not wonderful'. But by giving a response like this, and violating the maxim, B is implying irony. The implication generated by an untruthful and exaggerated statement is sarcasm; implication generated by an opposite statement from the one expected is irony. These meanings are possible through the deliberate violation of the conversational maxims and are called 'conversational implicatures' by Grice.

The insights provided by these theories of pragmatics have helped us to understand meaning as part of communication rather than as something abstract. They have also helped to analyse units of linguistic organization higher than the sentence, pairs of sentences taken as units, and sequences of sentences taken as texts, leading us to the analysis of meaning in connected language, i.e., discourse.

14.2 DISCOURSE ANALYSIS

As soon as we begin to study meaning in language in relation to context, we find that it is situated within two kinds of context. One is the **extra-linguistic**, i.e. the content of the external world. The other is the **intra-linguistic**, i.e. the linguistic context in which that piece of language occurs. So, for example, words occur within a sentential context, sentences occur within a context consisting of other sentences. In the analysis of language at the level of discourse, we are concerned with this intra-linguistic context.

Discourse is a level higher than that of the sentence. It includes all the other linguistic levels—sound, lexis, syntax. All these continue to make up a discourse. But here we must distinguish between the grammatical aspect and the semantic/pragmatic aspect of discourse. The former creates a text and the latter creates a discourse. In the former, words continue to form sentences, sentences combine to form a text. Just as there are rules for combination of words, there are certain relations between sentences and rules by which they may be related. These rules of sentence-connection create **cohesion** in the text. At the same time, these sentences are also utterances, i.e. they have a force which is vital for understanding their meaning, which are combined to create **coherence**. Thus we may distinguish between text and discourse in that text is created by sentence-cohesion and discourse is created by coherence. A discourse may be defined as a stretch of language-use which is coherent in its meaning. It will of course include grammar and cohesion. The following is an example of discourse which is both cohesive and coherent:

A : Can you go to Delhi tomorrow?
B : Yes, I can.

The interchange is cohesive because the second sentence does not repeat the whole of the first sentence. Instead of the whole sentence: 'I can go to Delhi tomorrow', B says only: 'I can', omitting the rest. This indicates that the second sentence is linked to the first in sequential order. It is also coherent because B has given an appropriate response to A from A's request. However, in the following example:

A : Can you go to Delhi tomorrow?
B : There is a general strike.

The two sentences are not cohesive because the second sentence is not linked to the first sentence in a grammatical sense. There is no repetition or obvious connection between the two sentences. But they are coherent, because B replies to A's request in a sentence which gives some information implying that it may not be possible to go to Delhi. Thus, this exchange is coherent but not cohesive.

In order to analyse discourse, it may be necessary to consider all aspects of language: the grammatical as well as the semantic and pragmatic (not forgetting the role of intonation). Grammatical forms which are used to link sentences and create cohesion can be of several kinds : logical connectors such as 'and', 'but'; conjuncts such as 'also', 'equally', 'furthermore', contrasts such as 'instead' and similarly, 'for', 'thus', substitutes for noun such as pro-forms 'he', 'she', 'they', 'one'; ellipsis, where some parts of a sentence are deleted; deixis, where one item points forward or backwards to what is being said or what has been said before. Deictic elements such as 'here', 'there', also indicate other references and are thus important in creating cohesion as well as discourse meaning.

Apart from grammatical features, discourse is constituted of features which are particular to the mode, tenor and field or domain of that discourse. The mode may be spoken or written. In spoken discourse there will be features of: inexplicitness, lack of clear sentence boundaries and sentence-completion, repetition, hesitation, interaction and maintenance features, e.g. 'well', 'you know', while in written discourse there will be features of explicitness, clear sentence boundaries and more complex sentences, formal features but no interactional and monitoring features. The tenor of discourse refers to features relating to the relationship between the speaker and the addressee in a given situation—these features reflect the formality or informality, degree of politeness, a personal or impersonal touch. Thus, if the relationship is a polite one, there will be respectful terms of address, e.g. 'Sir', and indirect requests rather than commands. If the relationship is one of familiarity, the features will include terms of friendship e.g. 'dear', direct requests and imperatives. Lastly, field or domain of discourse pertains to the area of activity to which that discourse belongs, e.g. whether the discourse is in the field of religion, science, law, journalism, advertising. In each field, the discourse will be characterized by a particular kind of vocabulary and sentence structure, e.g. sports commentary uses present tense; advertising uses many adjectives. Literary discourse often freely combines features from many kinds of discourse and occupies a different status from other types of discourse.

SUMMARY

Semantics is concerned with word and sentence meaning, pragmatics entails utterance meaning. An utterance can be defined as a word or sentence which is uttered by a speaker. The context of an utterance consists of: speaker, the sentence which is uttered, the act performed in the uttering of the sentence, and the hearer.

It is useful to distinguish between sentence meaning and utterance meaning, because meaning is more than the logical statement or the sense; it also contains the meaning intended by the speaker, expressed through the performance of the speech act. This meaning is the illocutionary force of the utterance. It is the action performed in the act of utterance, e.g. declaring, requesting, complaining.

It is also necessary to consider the Co-operative Principle that operates in speech communication. Under this principle, the maxims of quality, quantity, relevance and manner operate to make the communication meaningful. If one or several of these maxims are violated, implied meaning is generated. When we look at the meaning beyond the level of the sentence, we move to the level of discourse. Several sentences together make up an intra-linguistic context, which contains items such as words and sentences that are linked to each other by a system or reference. For instance, pronouns occurring later in the group of sentences would refer backwards to nouns which have been mentioned earlier. Similarly, articles, conjunctions, demonstratives etc. function as cohesive links in a set of sentences and make it a text. As distinct from this, coherence occurs when sentences are meaningfully linked to each other, in the presence or even absence of grammatical cohesion. Coherence creates a discourse, and field, mode and tenor are features that determine a particular discourse.

COMPREHENSION QUESTIONS

1. Why is it necessary to extend semantics to pragmatics?

2. Distinguish between sense and force in the following examples:

(a) Can you pass the salt?
(b) Do you want to sign here?
(c) I warn you not to be late.

3. Explain how the flouting of conversational maxims can lead to implicature.

4. Distinguish between cohesion and coherence.

CHAPTER 15

Principles of Lexicography

15.1 LEXICOLOGY AND DICTIONARY

Lexicology is the science or the set of theoretical principles that govern the production of a dictionary. Dictionary writing or lexicography is a professional activity aiming at the production of dictionaries. It has its own established practices. Dictionaries deal with the everchanging meaning, pronunciation and use of words. Lexicography covers both the processes related to observable phenomenon, i.e. words or lexis and the theoretical principles required to be followed to tackle or explain the meanings or use of words.

A dictionary is only a finished product, the result of a complex process. It is a reference book or list of words usually in an alphabetical order together with a guide to their meanings, pronunciation, spelling or equivalents in other languages or in simple words in the same languages.

15.2 THE LINGUISTIC BASIS OF LEXICOGRAPHY OR DICTIONARY COMPILATION

Dictionary writing is a complex process. It is not as simple as it sounds. A lexicographer must fully understand what exactly he means by the term 'word'. How are words related to their meanings? He has, therefore, to depend solely on some important principles of linguistics and concepts of semantics to do full justice to his job. Linguistic principles and semantic insights can be ignored by any writer of dictionaries only at his peril. Here are some general principles that a lexicographer must keep in mind:

1. The principle of descriptivism rather than prescriptivism. A writer of a dictionary has to **describe** words of a language (or a variety of that language). He has to describe the way the words **are** used, not as they **should** be used. A dictionary has to be descriptive, not normative or prescriptive. Since users would be interested in the pronunciation and spellings of words, a dictionary should preferably contain the correct spellings and pronunciation of the concerned words. This pronunciation can be recorded in symbols with the help of IPA (International

Phonetic Association) symbols* and well illustrated and explained diacritical marks. The reader may also, at times, like to know the history of a word or its etymology or its changing spellings and meanings. This can be either touched on in brief or kept apart for special dictionaries meant for the purpose. Dictionaries have, in many cases, to be bilingual as L_2 learners of any language go to the dictionary of L_1 language to look for equivalent words/expressions in their own language, i.e. L_1. Suitable synonyms in the same language are always an asset in any good dictionary.

2. Dictionaries vary in sizes and content. From pocket editions to large dictionaries consisting of several volumes (each volume consisting of more than a thousand pages), all types of dictionaries have been produced in different languages. Therefore, one has to select or delimit the scope of the dictionary. It may describe the whole vocabulary of the language (variety) in hand or a part of the vocabulary. Different dictionaries can cater to different groups/classes of words as a result of this selective coverage, e.g. a *Dictionary of Medical Terms*, a *Dictionary of Commercial Terms and Phraseology*, a *Dictionary of Philosophy*. Labour can also be usefully divided by having different dictionaries to deal with different aspects of language, viz. pronunciation, etymology, spellings, technical terminology (different types), idioms, dialects or varieties of the same language and so on.

3. Every dictionary has to develop its own code, a sort of meta-language for handling and presenting information. Different lexicographers have developed different concepts and practices for the purpose. One such example is the use of phonetic symbols to describe the pronunciation of words. These symbols, selected from the IPA list of separate symbols for separate sounds, converts speech into a sort of writing where you can 'read' as you 'write'. Orthographical description of words is generally misleading. Another example is the use of symbols like N., V., and Adj., for grammatical categories as a part of grammatical coding of various categories of words. Use of superscribed numerals for different semantic uses of the same word is another such device used by lexicographers. Different lexicographers develop or use their own metalanguage even though a lot of uniformity is being increasingly brought in as languages are breaking the man-made barriers across the world.

4. The writing of a dictionary involves a consideration of the clientele for which it is meant. 'Who is the dictionary meant for?' is an important question that every lexicographer must answer before starting his work. Ever since the start of the writing of dictionaries, this question has always been raised. Samuel Johnson asked it in 1747 and gave a didactic answer: 'The value of a work must be estimated by its use. It is not enough that a dictionary delights the critic, unless at the same time it instructs the learners'.

* There are other ways too but IPA symbols are being increasingly accepted by lexicographers.

Dictionary writing is, thus, a very complex activity. Apart from the huge labour involved in the process, a dictionary writer has to be aware of all the principles involved in compiling this important work. He has to keep an eye on the target audience, their needs and situations and the various operations involved in the process.

15.3 VARIOUS TYPES OF DICTIONARIES

The term 'dictionary' generally includes any reference book giving information under topics arranged alphabetically, such as a dictionary of music or a dictionary of biography. The English word 'dictionary' is an adaptation of the Medieval Latin 'dictionarium' or 'dictionarius', meaning 'a repertory of phrases or words (dictiones)'. Since several years the word 'dictionary' has been used in the titles of works **explaining words**. In contrast to the encyclopaedias, which summarise what is known in all branches of knowledge, dictionaries deal with the individual words of a language or with certain specified classes of them. Dictionaries present information about the spelling, pronunciation and meaning of their entry words in some systematic way—usually in alphabetical order. Larger dictionaries offer additional items of information about synonyms, levels of usage, and etymologies and often provide quotations and pictures.

Here are some important types of dictionaries in use:

General purpose dictionaries

Even though a dictionary is compiled with a particular target audience in mind yet, by convention, a dictionary has come to be thought of as a book containing an alphabetical list of words, their meanings, uses, pronunciation etc. Such a dictionary is a General Purpose Dictionary which is meant for all users of the language in question. Dictionaries of this type are available in several languages in several different sizes varying from a pocket book size to one consisting of several volumes. The 'abridged' dictionaries do not have as much information as the full sized ones have.

Scholarly dictionaries

Apart from the dictionaries meant for practical use, there are the scholarly dictionaries. These dictionaries are meant for specialists in the particular language and are complete in all respects. An example of such a scholarly dictionary is the *Thesaurus Linguage Latinae*, edited in Germany. *The Oxford English Dictionary* is another such work popular with the scholars.

Specialised dictionaries

Specialized dictionaries are those dictionaries which deal in detail with just one special area of lexical study, e.g. etymology, pronunciation, and usage. *Roget's Thesaurus*, for example is a dictionary of synonyms. Similarly, *Everman's English Pronouncing Dictionary* by Daniel Jones is a dictionary dealing only with the pronunciation of words. These dictionaries are meant for those users of language who specialise in their selected fields of linguistics studies.

Dialect dictionaries

Since every language has its own varieties depending on the region, writers of different languages have brought out dictionaries pertaining to their particular dialects. Some such dictionaries are available in various English dialects too.

Technical dictionaries

There are some dictionaries that deal with the technical terms of some particular disciplines. Dictionaries like, *A Dictionary of Computing*, *A Glossary of Law Terms*, *A Glossary of Medical Terms*, etc. belong to this category. In such dictionaries the lexicographers have to refer to particular specialists in the field or some various thinkers who may happen to differ on the interpretation of certain technical terms.

15.4 LINGUISTIC FEATURES OF A DICTIONARY

Any user of any dictionary must be fully conversant with all the linguistic features of the dictionary he is using. We now list a few major dictionaries which are in popular use and their linguistic features:

(i) *Everyman's Pronouncing Dictionary* (14th ed.) by Daniel Jones

1. It contains over 59,000 words in international phonetic transcription.
2. The pronunciation of words recorded in this dictionary is based on the usage current among native speakers (RP) of the middle generations.
3. The variants of words are given in brackets.
4. Many entries include pronunciations which contain an Italic symbol. This symbol stands for a sound that is being optionally used by speakers.
5. The degrees of word accent are shown and weak syllables are unmarked.
6. The pronunciations of all plurals of nouns are shown under the singulars. Degrees of adjective and inflected forms of verbs are given under simple forms from which they are derived.
7. A number of foreign words and proper names are included in this dictionary.
8. An attempt is made to represent interjections and hesitation noises generally used in English by using the following symbols:

   /Y̊/ French /y/ but without voice

   /n̥/ voiceless /n/

   /ə̃/ nasalized /ə/
9. The terms 'weak' and 'strong' are used for alternative pronunciations possible for grammatical items in connected speech.
10. Detailed information about consonant clusters and linking /r/ is given.
11. A certain number of common abbreviations are included and listed in alphabetical order according to the letters composing them.

(ii) *Advanced Learner's Dictionary* (4th ed.) by A.S. Hornby

1. The dictionary contains a large number of entries, more than in any other similar dictionary.

2. The pronunciation of every word, using IPA symbols, has been given in phonemic transcription. The symbols used conform to the symbols used in *Everyman's Pronouncing Dictionary* (14th ed.) by Daniel Jones.
3. Several possible meanings of each word are given and in order to distinguish between different shades of meaning, sentences (in full or half) have been given where required.
4. Abbreviations like V. (verb), N. (noun), Adj. (adjective), Adv. (adverb) have been given to classify each word into a particular class.
5. Use of prepositions with head words have been discussed in detail.
6. At several places both American and British pronunciations and meanings have been given.
7. Photographs or diagrams of some words have been given to make the meanings clear.
8. The dictionary contains a list of phonetic symbols used in it on its title page (inside cover).
9. It also contains a detailed account of the sentence patterns in its introduction part.
10. A number of appendices appear with the dictionary. These include irregular verbs, common abbreviations, affixes, numerical expressions, weights and measures, geographical and common names and list of Shakespeare's works.
11. Use of punctuation marks has been discussed in detail.
12. The plurals of words, their past participle forms (if any) have also been given.

(iii) Collins Cobuild Essential English Dictionary

1. This dictionary contains a large number of entries arranged alphabetically, with no notice being taken of capital letters, hyphens or spaces between words.
2. Phrasal verbs are put in paragraphs immediately after the simple verb, e.g. close, close down, close in, closed.
3. Phrases are printed in bold type in the entry for the most important word in the phrase.
4. Cross-references are also given in this dictionary, e.g. if we have to find the entry of **face value**, then we can find it under the entry of **value.**
5. The spelling for each form of word is given in bold letters at the beginning of the entry.
6. The pronunciation of each word is given after the first form of the word.
7. Abbreviations like V. (verb), N. (noun), Adj. (Adjective), Adv. (Adverb), have been given to classify each word into a particular class.
8. Words are explained in simple English.
9. The words in the dictionary contain grammatical information given about them in an extra column.
10. In addition to grammar codes, the extra column also has information about how and when one should use a word.

11. More information on study pages is given where the main grammatical categories such as Adj., phrasal verbs and pronouns are dealt with.
12. In this dictionary a guide is given to the pronunciation of International Phonetic Alphabet (IPA). Several accents of English have been discussed but RP variety, it is stated, is perhaps the most widely used as a norm for teaching purposes.

SUMMARY

Lexicology is the science or the set of theoretical principles that govern the production of a dictionary. Dictionary writing is a complex process. It is a reference book or a list of words usually in an alphabetical order, together with a guide to their meanings, pronunciation, spellings or equivalents in other languages or in simple words in the same languages.

A lexicographer should keep in mind the following principles:

1. A dictionary writer should be descriptive, not prescriptive.
2. Dictionaries vary in sizes and content according to the audience that uses them.
3. Every dictionary has to develop its own code, a sort of metalanguage for handling and presenting information.
4. A dictionary writer must keep an eye on the needs of the clientele for whom it is meant.

There are various types of dictionaries, e.g. general purpose dictionaries, scholarly dictionaries, specialised dictionaries, dialect dictionaries and technical dictionaries. Every dictionary has its own particular linguistic features which every user of the dictionary should be aware of.

COMPREHENSION QUESTIONS

1. What is lexicology? What is the linguistic basis of lexicography? Explain.
2. Enumerate and explain the theoretical principles that should guide a lexicographer.
3. Write an essay on various types of dictionaries.
4. What do you understand by the term linguistic features of a dictionary? Discuss the linguistic features of any one dictionary you use.
5. Fill up the blanks:
   (a) ______________ is the set of theoretical principles that govern the production of a dictionary.
   (b) A lexicographer has to be ______________ (descriptive/prescriptive).

(c) Dictionaries vary in content and sizes (________) (True or False).

(d) A dictionary has its own code, a sort of ________________ for handling and presenting information.

(e) A dictionary is different from an encyclopaedia which tries to summarise what is known in ________________ branches of knowledge (all/some).

References

Abercrombie, D., *Elements of General Phonetics,* Edinburgh: Edinburgh University Press, 1967.

Akmajian, H. et al., *Linguistics—An Introduction to Language and Communication,* 5th ed., New Delhi: Prentice-Hall of India, 1996.

Austin, J.L., *How to Do Things with Words.* Cambridge, Mass: Harvard University Press, 1960.

Bloch, B. and Trager, G., *Outline of Linguistic Analysis.* Baltimore: Waverly Press, 1942.

Bloomfield, L., *Language.* New Delhi: Motilal Banarsidas, 1963.

Bolinger, D., *Aspects of Language.* New York: Harcourt Brace Jovanovich, 1975.

Brown, G. and Yule, G., *The Study of Language.* Cambridge: Cambridge University Press, 1980.

Chomsky, N., *Syntactic Structures.* The Hague: Mouton, 1957.

——, *Aspects of the Theory of Syntax.* Cambridge: Cambridge University Press, 1965.

Corder, S.P., *Introducing Applied Linguistics.* Harmondsworth: Penguin, 1973.

Crystal, D., *Linguistics.* Harmondsworth: Penguin, 1978.

Derbyshrine, A.E., *A Description of English.* New Delhi: Arnold Heinemann, 1967.

de Saussure, F., *Course in General Linguistics.* 1916. Translated by Wade Baskin, New York: Philosophical Library, 1959.

Firth, J.R., *Papers in Linguistics 1934–1951.* Oxford: Oxford University Press, 1957.

Gleason, H.A., *An Introduction to Descriptive Linguistics.* New Delhi: Oxford and IBH, 1970.

Hall, R.A. Jr., *Introductory Linguistics.* Delhi: Motialal Banarsidas, 1969.

Halliday, M.A.K., *Language as a Social Semiotic.* London: Edward Arnold, 1978.

Hockett, C., *A Course in Modern Linguistics.* New Delhi: Oxford and IBH, 1970.

Jacobs, R. and Rosenbaum, P.S., *English Transformational Grammar.* Waltham, Mass: Blaisdell, 1969.

Jesperson, O., *Essentials of English Grammar.* London: Allen and Unwin, 1933.

Jones, D., *Outline of English Phonetics.* Cambridge: Cambridge University Press, 1914.

Leech, G.N., *Semantics*. Harmondsworth: Penguin, 1981.

Lyons, J., *New Horizons in Linguistics*. Harmondsworth: Penguin, 1970.

______, *An Introduction to Theoretical Linguistics*. Cambridge: Cambridge University Press, 1971.

______, *Language and Linguistics*. Cambridge: Cambridge University Press, 1981.

______, *Chomsky*. London: Fontana, 1975.

Ogden, C.R. and Richards, I.A., *The Meaning of Meaning*. London: Routledge and Kegan Paul, 1923.

Palmer, F., *Grammar*. London: Longman and ELBS, 1985.

Quirk, R. and Greenbaum, S., *A University Grammar of English*. London: Longman and ELBS, 1982.

Robins, R.H., *General Linguistics—An Introductory Survey.* London: Longman, 1985.

______, *A Short History of Linguistics.* London: Longman, 1969.

Sapir, E., *Language*. 1921. also in Sapir, E. *Selected Writings*, Berkeley: University of California Press, 1949.

Stageberg, N.C., *An Introductory English Grammar*. New York: Holt Saunders, 1983.

Verma, S.K. and Krishnaswamy, N., *Modern Linguistics—An Introduction.* New Delhi: Oxford University Press, 1989.

Wardaugh, R., *An Introduction to Linguistics*. New York: McGraw-Hill, 1972.

Zandvoort, R.W., *A Handbook of English Grammar,* 7th ed., London: Longman and ELBS, 1978.

Index